English Language Learners
Teacher's Handbook

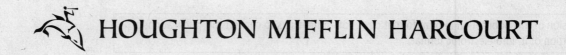

HOUGHTON MIFFLIN HARCOURT

Photo Credits

Placement Key: (r) right, (l) left, (c) center, (t) top, (b) bottom, (bg) background

3 Jupiterimages/Getty Images; 6 (tl) ©Digital Vision/Getty Images; 7 (tr) Comstock/Getty Images

All other photos are property of Houghton Mifflin Harcourt.

Acknowledgments

Excerpt from *Texas Write Source Writing and Grammar Teacher's Edition, Grade 11* by David Keper, Patrick Sebranek and Verne Meyer, Consulting Author Gretchen Bernabei, illustrated by Chris Krenzke. Copyright © 2012 by Houghton Mifflin Harcourt Publishing Company. Reprinted by permission of Houghton Mifflin Harcourt Publishing Company.

Printed in the U.S.A.

ISBN   978-0-547-89334-1

13   0982   21 20 19 18 17 16 15 14

4500516378   B C D E F G

Contents

Professional Development

Resources

English Language Learners Today

▶ Background

According to the U.S. Census Bureau (2011), nearly eleven million children between the ages of five and seventeen speak a language other than English at home. An English language proficiency test, given when these students enter school (and repeated annually to assess their progress in English), determines whether they are designated as English language learners (ELLs). ELLs are the fastest-growing group of students in the classroom (National Clearinghouse for English Language Acquisition 2010).

Title III, Part A of the No Child Left Behind Act requires ELLs to meet the same challenging standards that non-ELLs are expected to meet (U.S. Department of Education 2002). Each state and district must provide effective programs to help ELLs overcome language barriers and achieve proficiency in reading/language arts, mathematics, and science. The Common Core State Standards adopted by many states raise the bar yet higher.

> **" Mastery of academic language is arguably the single most important determinant of academic success for individual students. "**
>
> **—David J. Francis et al. (2006), p. 7**

In order to achieve academic success, ELLs need to master the English used for everyday conversations (social language), the English used for classroom management (instructional language), and the English used in each of the content areas (academic language). Many ELLs are able to communicate well in English in social situations but have not yet acquired the specialized English language proficiency needed to understand grade-level academic content and participate in classroom work. Often, these students are not able to understand complex texts, participate in class discussions, or do well on tests.

▶ Programs for ELLs

Educators have developed many types of programs to help ELLs acquire both English language proficiency and content knowledge. These programs may be grouped according to their goals (English language development only or English language development and content-area learning) and their language of instruction (English only or English and students' first language).

> **" The key issue is not finding a program that works for all children and all localities, but rather finding a set of program components that works for the children in the community of interest, given that community's goals, demographics, and resources. "**
>
> **—Diane August & Kenji Hakuta (1998), p. 54**

Name of Program	Program Goal	Language of Instruction
English as a Second Language (ESL)	Development of English language skills:	English
English Language Development (ELD)	• listening	
English for Speakers of Other Languages (ESOL)	• speaking • reading • writing	
Self-Contained ESL	Development of English language skills and content-area knowledge	English
Structured English Immersion (SEI)		
Sheltered English Instruction (Models: SIOP, CALLA, SDAIE)		
Newcomer	Intensive English language and literacy development, sometimes with content instruction (for recently arrived immigrant students, often those who have limited prior formal education)	English or English and first language
Transitional Bilingual Education (TBE)	Development of English language skills and content-area knowledge through use of the first language, with transition to English-only instruction	English and first language
Developmental Bilingual Education	Development of language skills and content knowledge in two languages	English and first language
Two-Way Bilingual Education Dual–Language Immersion	Development of language skills and content knowledge in two languages, with students from two (or more) different language groups	English and a second (target) language

▶ ELLs in Mainstream Classrooms

ELLs are often taught in regular classrooms, rather than in special programs. They bring to the classroom diverse skills and language proficiencies, and it becomes the responsibility of the classroom teacher to meet their varied needs. Not only must ELLs join other students in achieving high standards, they must also be prepared for state and standardized tests.

How can the classroom teacher meet the needs of ELLs along with other diverse learners? The first step is to find out as much as possible about each ELL.

▶ First–Language Literacy and Exposure to English

Approximately eighty percent of ELLs in the classroom are Spanish speaking. Chinese (Mandarin or Cantonese), Vietnamese, French/Haitian Creole, Hindi, and Korean are among the other first languages of ELLs. Note, however, that most ELLs are not immigrants. Eighty-five percent of ELLs were born in the United States (U.S. Department of Education 2008), but they may have had little exposure to English before enrolling in kindergarten or first grade.

Thus, ELLs come with a wide variety of prior linguistic experiences. Answers to questions such as the following can help educators understand difficulties these children may encounter and plan reading instruction accordingly.

- **How well do children know their first language? Can they read and write in the first language?** Literacy in the first language makes developing literacy in English much easier.

- **How much exposure have children had to English?** Low proficiency in oral English is a barrier to reading comprehension and writing proficiency.

- **What are the alphabetic, phonological, and grammatical structures of the children's first language?** Similar alphabets, sound systems, and grammar patterns facilitate transfer from first-language reading to English reading.

> " **Ideally, teachers should be aware of what students know and can do in their primary language so they can help them apply it to tasks in English.** "
>
> —Claude Goldenberg (2008), p. 9

▶ ELL Proficiency Levels

There is a significant difference between a newly arrived, zero-level English language learner and one whose language is nearly equivalent to that of a student whose primary language is English. One of the first things teachers must do when ELLs are placed in their classrooms is find out each student's English language proficiency (ELP) level.

ELLs should be tested for English language proficiency on arrival in a new school district, and annually thereafter. If you do not have a student's test score, you can use the chart on page 5 to do your own informal assessment. Once you know what language proficiency levels your ELLs have, take some time to become familiar with the characteristics of those levels. Don't expect ELLs to understand or produce language that is beyond their proficiency level. The third column of the chart will help you differentiate your questions and prompts according to students' language proficiencies.

ELP Level	Student Understands and Can Use ...	Student Can ...	Teacher Prompts
Beginning	• language about basic concrete needs and simple routine experiences • high-frequency words and memorized language • sight words, phrases, and short sentences • pictures, graphics, and nonverbal communication	**Listening:** begin to understand everyday language and classroom routines **Speaking:** respond to questions nonverbally or with one- or two-word answers **Reading:** recognize familiar words in a text; read some common environmental print **Writing:** copy words and short phrases; use invented spelling to write common words and short predictable phrases	• point • show me • draw • listen • choose • match • mime • act out
Low Intermediate	• language about familiar topics and situations • general vocabulary and some academic vocabulary • expanded sentences	**Listening:** understand language of daily classroom interaction **Speaking:** use phrases and short, simple sentences; ask simple questions **Reading:** understand simple text when background knowledge and visual or graphic support exist **Writing:** write simple sentences with many grammar and spelling errors	• yes/no questions • either/or questions • complete an open-ended sentence • name • list • categorize • label
High Intermediate	• language about concrete and abstract situations • academic language and some technical vocabulary	**Listening:** understand most daily speech but not all academic language **Speaking:** communicate well in social situations with some grammatical errors; ask questions for clarification but has difficulty with academic concepts **Reading:** read independently with support **Writing:** write independently but continues to make grammatical errors; write texts that are more coherent, but the texts will lack complexity	• what happens/happened • list causes • describe/tell about things • compare/contrast things • restate • give an example • give an opinion • define • explain • recall • summarize • role-play
Proficient	• a variety of longer oral and written texts • academic and technical vocabulary and expressions	**Listening:** understand social and academic language, including idioms and some technical language **Speaking:** carry on conversations on social and academic topics with little or no support **Reading:** read and understand grade-level text with minimal support **Writing:** write with a variety of sentence structures, clarity, and good organization, with minimal errors	• why/why not • describe/tell about events • compare/contrast ideas/events • explain how • what if ... • support opinion • define • explain causes • defend • debate • examine • analyze • create • evaluate

▶ Profiles of English Language Learners

Combining linguistic factors with the individual factors that all students bring to school means there is wide variation among ELLs in any classroom. Every ELL, like every other child, is an individual. Certain characteristics, however, are common among many ELLs (Freeman & Freeman 2009). The following fictional profiles will illustrate some of those characteristics.

Hadessah, age 10 (Recently arrived, with rigorous formal schooling)

Hadessah is a well-mannered, quiet, and conscientious student who arrived in the United States about a year ago. She reads and writes almost at grade level and has basic oral fluency in English, but she never speaks up in class. If called on, she mumbles very softly and is virtually incomprehensible. Hadessah had a rigorous academic schedule at her school in Lebanon, including classical Arabic and French. Her parents are both professionals who know several languages and are very involved in their daughter's school life.

Instructional Considerations

Teachers can guide students, such as Hadessah, to understand how their first or second language affects their acquisition of English. For example, some primary language sounds, words, and grammatical structures transfer directly to English, while others will cause ELLs to make errors when learning English.

Miguel, age 13 (Recently arrived, with limited formal schooling)

Miguel looks tall for sixth grade, because he should be in eighth. Unfortunately, there is no newcomer program in the school district his family just moved to from the Dominican Republic. Miguel lacks consistent previous schooling and knows very little English, so the district placed him in sixth grade. Miguel is polite and very quiet, almost withdrawn. He is anxious to learn and very eager to please. His parents do not speak any English, but they want him to succeed.

Instructional Considerations

Students with inconsistent prior schooling face the challenge of trying to learn reading and writing skills and acquire content knowledge while they are learning a new language. Their families want them to succeed but are often unable to support them in school. Teachers need to take advantage of every possible source of support they can find for these students and their families.

Sodka, age 8 (Potential long–term English language learner)

Sodka is the first person in her Cambodian family to be born in the United States. She knew very little English when she started kindergarten, but now, in third grade, she speaks English fluently. Sodka has attended several different schools, where she did not always have ESL support. She likes school, but she has great difficulty with reading and writing. Her parents speak some English but can't help her with schoolwork because of their long work hours and lack of English literacy skills.

Instructional Considerations

ELLs who do not have sufficient, appropriate instruction or support when they begin schooling in English are often in danger of falling behind in literacy development. By the time they are in fourth or fifth grade, they may be several years behind grade level in reading and writing, and at risk of becoming "long-term ELLs."

Long–Term English Language Learners

Long-term English language learners are those who have been in school in the United States for at least seven years but are still below grade level in reading and math (Freeman & Freeman 2009). These students appear fluent in spoken English but do not have the academic language proficiency needed for success with grade-level academic tasks. Identifying potential long-term ELLs in the early grades and providing the intensive academic language support they need could help more of them succeed.

The ELL–Friendly Classroom

▶ General Principles

Keeping a few general principles in mind will ensure that your classroom is a place where English language learners can succeed. First, create a supportive, low-stress environment where ELLs are more willing to take risks and experiment with their new language. There are multiple ways to do this: encouraging other students to "adopt" a newly arrived ELL, incorporating ELLs' first languages and cultures into the classroom, and making sure that peer tutoring becomes a two-way process.

Second, create an environment in which ELLs participate in all activities and profit from every minute of the day. To encourage ELLs to participate, it's important to enlist the help of bilingual classroom aides, volunteer tutors, peer helpers, media specialists, and parents. Materials in students' first languages, bilingual dictionaries, and visuals will also provide support for ELLs in the classroom.

Third, create an environment in which ELLs can succeed at the tasks given to them. Repeated lack of success at an assigned task is especially frustrating for ELLs because they often know they could do the task if they could only produce the language needed. There are multiple ways to help ELLs succeed with language, such as modifying assignments, adapting teaching strategies, using the first language when possible, utilizing a variety of resources, and adapting assessment procedures. The Sheltered Instruction Observation Protocol model, or SIOP (Echevarria, Vogt, & Short 2012), is a useful resource for teachers who want to modify their teaching strategies to create this kind of environment.

▶ Tips for Designing an ELL–Friendly Classroom

Here are some simple ideas you can use to create a supportive classroom environment for English language learners:

- Create a Welcome Book for newly arrived ELLs containing names and pictures of classmates and school staff, a map of the school with important locations labeled, basic school vocabulary, and space for additional entries. ELLs can make individualized additions to the book when working with their fluent English-speaking peers.

- Fill your classroom with visuals. Label everything in English and perhaps other languages. Make a word wall to display current vocabulary and refer to it often. Hang photos and posters with labels, illustrating each new topic students learn about. Post classroom rules and routines, and refer to them daily.

- Pair ELLs with English-speaking "buddies" who can help them navigate the school, understand rules and procedures, practice vocabulary, and adapt to American culture.

School Map

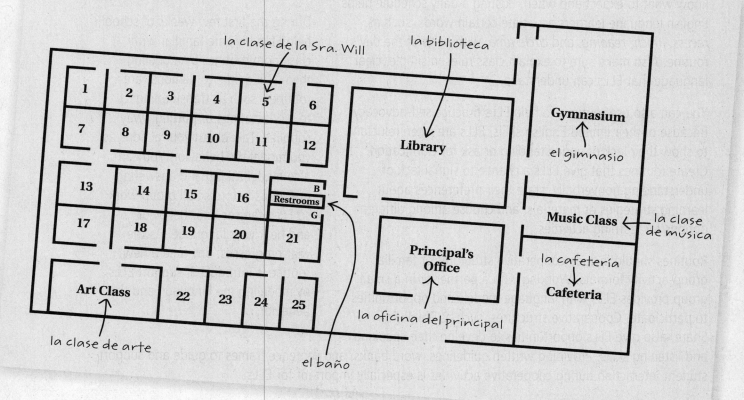

la clase de la Sra. Will

la biblioteca

1 2 3 4 5 6

7 8 9 10 11 12

13 14 15 16

B
Restrooms
G

17 18 19 20 21

Art Class 22 23 24 25

Library

Principal's Office

Gymnasium

el gimnasio

Music Class ← la clase de música

la cafetería

Cafeteria

la oficina del principal

la clase de arte

el baño

- Give your students access to a variety of books at different reading levels. Borrow books from the library to supplement your classroom library. For beginning ELLs, books in which the pictures support the meaning of the text are very helpful. Include books for certain times of the year, and those that highlight different countries and cultures. Include bilingual or first-language books, if possible. Read aloud to students frequently.

- Arrange student desks in groups of four, with students who speak English as their first language and ELLs in each group whenever possible.

- Keep manipulatives on hand for playing language games. Word tiles, sentence frame strips, and memory games are tools that support students' English language development in an engaging, hands-on way.

- Make music a part of every day. Singing songs is an effective way to learn a new language, especially if students act out parts of the song while singing.

▶ Using Routines and Cooperative Structures

Routines are another way to support ELLs in your classroom. When you establish a daily routine with your students, they know what to expect and when. Posting a daily schedule helps English language learners associate certain words, such as *recess*, *lunch*, *reading*, and *circle time*, with parts of the day's routine. Also make sure to explain class rules in simple, clear language that ELLs can understand.

You can also use routines to help ELLs practice self-advocacy. Because of their limited English skills, ELLs are often reluctant to show their lack of understanding or ask for clarification. Create routines that give ELLs a chance to signal lack of understanding nonverbally, state their preferences about learning strategies or materials, and choose among different options for learning activities.

Routines should include cooperative structures or familiar group-activity formats. Working with a partner or in a small group provides ELLs with language models and opportunities to participate. Cooperative structures, such as Think-Pair-Share, also give ELLs opportunities to develop their speaking and listening skills. Providing written guidelines, word banks, and sentence frames to guide and support student interaction during cooperative activities is especially important for ELLs.

Finally, it is important to use preteaching routines to prepare ELLs for lessons. A single short activity can build background, preview the lesson, and present new vocabulary in context.

Modeling Classroom Routines

During the first few weeks of school, help ELLs become familiar with classroom routines by modeling them. Take time to demonstrate routines, such as transitioning to work stations or putting away supplies. Talk about your actions as you model the behavior. You can also model asking and answering questions before small group work so ELLs can see your behavior and hear your language. As the year progresses, any time a new routine is introduced, support ELLs by modeling the language and the behavior.

Honoring and Incorporating Culture and Community

Students who come from different countries and cultures can enrich your classroom. You can honor and incorporate your ELLs' cultures and backgrounds through procedures such as these:

- Label everything in the classroom in students' first languages as well as in English. Enlist students' help for this task.
- Let ELLs be the experts by asking each student to teach the class a new word in his or her first language once a week.
- Include elements of your students' cultures in your classroom. Post pictures of their home countries, or display props that represent their homelands, along with symbols of the United States.

Most of your English language learners will be eager to teach others about their language and customs, but some may not wish to have their culture or background highlighted. In that case, consider making your classroom a multicultural space that honors many different countries and cultures.

▶ Creating a Home–School Partnership

Parents of ELLs can face daunting obstacles, such as the inability to understand English, unfamiliarity with the school system, and differences in cultural norms, as they try to become informed about or involved with their children's school. Educators can help parents and other responsible family members by nourishing the home-school connection with non-English-speaking parents in ways such as these:

1. Decide what's important before you send it home. A folder full of information in English can be overwhelming for parents who don't understand the language. If something is very important or urgent (e.g., the need for medical records, a signature), establish in advance a way to indicate this on the paper (perhaps with a special symbol).

2. Write a few words or phrases on a test or assignment that the student did well on, and send that home. Use stickers and icons and, if possible, a few words in the student's first language. Have students translate the comments for their parents as homework.

> **Research supports the importance of parental involvement for improved student achievement, better school attendance, and reduced dropout rates regardless of socioeconomic background or ethnicity.**
>
> —M. Beatriz Arias and M. Morillo-Campbell (2008), p. 1

3. Send home a book in the student's first language on the theme being studied in class. Suggest that students read and discuss the book with family members.

4. Establish a dialogue journal. Once a week, send a notebook home with your students containing a sentence or two about the student's work in both simple English and, if possible, the student's first language. Encourage family members to respond.

5. Try to learn a few words in the student's first language. Your student's parents will appreciate the effort, and you'll appreciate how challenging it can be to learn a second language!

6. If your school has a large percentage of students of a single language group, consider hiring a parent liaison or engaging one or more of the bilingual parents as a volunteer. A bilingual parent liaison can help with phone calls, parent-teacher conferences, translations of important materials, and attendance issues. This benefits everyone—students, families, teachers, and the school.

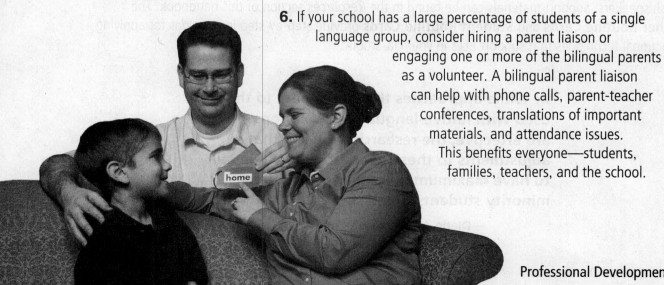

③ Effective Teaching Practices for ELLs

▶ **ELL Best Practices**

Many teaching strategies that mainstream teachers already use, such as activating background knowledge or using cooperative learning, are helpful to ELLs. However, in order to serve ELLs effectively, it is important to adapt these strategies using techniques that specifically support language learning.

Ten instructional strategies for ELLs are identified and described in this section. These **ELL Best Practices** include techniques that benefit ELLs of all proficiency levels and reflect what research tells us about how they learn.

❶ Make Language and Content Comprehensible

❷ Provide Hands-On Activities

❸ Promote Oral Language Development

❹ Integrate Language Objectives into Every Lesson

❺ Scaffold Instruction to Meet ELLs' Needs

❻ Encourage Cooperative Learning

❼ Draw from Student Experiences and Culture

❽ Develop Academic Language and Critical Thinking

❾ Activate and Evaluate Background Knowledge

❿ Build In Ongoing Assessment

Most of the ELL Best Practices, and the accompanying techniques provided for each one, can be used with all students, whether the students are learning English, have special needs, or are fluent English speakers. Support materials can be found in the *Resources* section of this handbook. The **Teacher Routine Cards** and **Student Routine Cards** provide step-by-step instructions for applying instructional techniques that support ELLs in your classroom.

> **❝ ... While approaches that are similar to those used with native-language populations are effective, the research suggests that adjustments to these approaches are needed to have maximum benefit with language-minority students. ❞**
>
> **—Diane August & Tim Shanahan (2006), p. 9**

ELL BEST PRACTICE ❶   Make Language and Content Comprehensible

Certain techniques can make language and content more comprehensible so that all English language learners will understand what is being taught. For example, if a teacher models the action while saying, "Please put your book on the shelf," all students in the classroom will know exactly what they should do.

Teachers can provide four types of support to ELLs to make language and content comprehensible:

1. visual (e.g., providing pictures of new vocabulary words)

2. auditory (e.g., thinking aloud as you work on decoding a word)

3. tactile (e.g., giving students letter tiles to form rhyming words)

4. linguistic (e.g., adjusting the language of instruction so each student hears and can respond to language at or slightly above his or her proficiency level)

Making Content Comprehensible

Here are some suggestions for helping to make language and content comprehensible:

- Use objects, actions, gestures, and visuals to demonstrate what you are teaching.
- Model and role-play activities before asking students to do them.
- Provide frequent examples to clarify concepts.
- Check regularly for student comprehension.
- Encourage students to ask for clarification.
- Create a unique sign or gesture for students to use when they don't understand.

 For activities to help make language and content comprehensible, see "Step-Up Questioning," **Teacher Routine Card 1**; "Cognates Choo-Choo Train," **Teacher Routine Card 7**; and "Teach Academic Vocabulary," **Teacher Routine Card 9,** found in the *Resources*.

ELL BEST PRACTICE ❷ Provide Hands–On Activities

Hands-on activities give students the opportunity to learn through manipulating objects, performing physical tasks, and conducting experiments. This opportunity is very helpful in classrooms where students have varied academic backgrounds and English proficiency levels. For ELLs, hands-on activities can provide a meaningful context that helps make the language associated with the activity more memorable.

Some additional benefits of hands-on learning for ELLs include:

- Physical activity can make the classroom environment seem more inviting.
- Learning can be seen as more interactive and motivating.
- Higher-order thinking and understanding of complex ideas and concepts can be facilitated.

Another benefit is that hands-on activities can free the teacher to conduct ongoing assessment. Once you have set up the classroom for a hands-on activity, you are free to walk around the room to check on and assist individual students. You may wish to create a mini-rubric, such as the one below, to use as an informal assessment of student work.

Student can...	Yulia	Manon	Suleyca	Felix
express ideas orally when prompted				
write words or sentences about the activity				
listen to directions and understand what to do				
read words associated with activity				

For activities with hands-on elements, see "Cognates Choo-Choo Train," **Teacher Routine Card 7,** and "Teach Academic Vocabulary," **Teacher Routine Card 9,** found in the *Resources*.

> ❝[With hands-on activities] abstract concepts become meaningful, transferable, and retained because they are attached to performance of an activity.❞
>
> —S. E. Cooperstein & E. Kocevar-Weidinger (2004), p. 141

ELL BEST PRACTICE ❸   Promote Oral Language Development

Teachers can best serve ELLs by creating opportunities to practice oral language in the classroom every day. The teacher's role is to create an interactive environment for ELLs that includes classroom discussions, cooperative learning, partner work, and student-teacher conferences.

If some students are reluctant to produce and exchange oral language, first steps can be taken one-on-one, with a partner or with the teacher. Later, as students feel more comfortable, they can work in larger groups and participate in class discussions.

> ❝ **Language learning is not a passive process; it is facilitated through production and interaction, and therefore, depends heavily on the ability to practice and produce language, especially in academic settings.** ❞
>
> —David J. Francis et al. (2006), p. 27

When interacting with students one-on-one, such as during writing conferences, teachers can accept students' one-word responses but help them expand language production by modeling longer responses. Depending on their proficiency levels, ELLs might be encouraged to respond to questions in complete sentences or explain how they knew the answer to a question.

Small-group activities can be structured to include the use of sentence frames and word banks to ensure that students at all proficiency levels can participate. If pairs or groups will report back to the class, provide guidelines for doing so.

For more ways to promote oral language development, see "Step-Up Questioning," **Teacher Routine Card 1**; "Respond to Reading," **Teacher Routine Card 2**; "Pick a Side," **Teacher Routine Card 3**; and "Pop-Up," **Teacher Routine Card 6,** found in the *Resources*. All **Student Routine Cards** found in the *Resources* support small-group interaction.

ELL BEST PRACTICE ❹   Integrate Language Objectives into Every Lesson

English language learners benefit from understanding the language objectives for each lesson in which they are participating. When a teacher reads and explains the day's language objectives, along with the content-area objectives, it focuses ELLs' attention on the language they'll use to master the content.

Teachers can use the following tips when writing language objectives for content-area lessons:

- First, ask: *What language will my students need to know and to use in order to achieve the content-area objectives?*

- Then choose target words, structures, and skills by thinking of "language" in terms of vocabulary (especially academic vocabulary), language structures or functions, and literacy skills.

- For each content-area objective, write language objectives using short sentences and student-friendly language.

Content-Area Objective	Language to Know and to Use	Language Objectives
Reading: Identify the story structure of a text.	Vocabulary: *plot, setting, characters, resolution, beginning, middle, ending* Language Structures: logical sequences using the transition words *first, then, next, finally* Literacy Skills: identify story elements	Students will be able to … • define and use the following words: *setting, characters, plot, resolution.* • write a story-retelling paragraph using the transition words *first, then, next, finally.* • explain a story's structure to a partner.

For support with integrating language objectives, see "Review Content and Language Objectives," **Teacher Routine Card 4,** found in the *Resources*.

> ❝**During English language development time, the focus is clearly on language. When teachers try to merge English language development with academics, it becomes easy to lose track of the dual objectives and focus more on teaching reading or mathematics or science than on teaching academic English.**❞
>
> —**Russell Gersten et al. (2007), p. 18**

ELL BEST PRACTICE ⑤   Scaffold Instruction to Meet ELLs' Needs

Teachers are frequently told to "differentiate instruction" for their students. *Differentiating* means adjusting instruction to provide for individual differences, whether the adjustments affect the materials, the assignments, or the method of presenting information. Scaffolding is a way to differentiate instruction and language demands for ELLs while addressing students' diverse background knowledge, literacy levels, and skills. The term *scaffolding* is borrowed from the building trades, where physical scaffolds help to support a building until it can stand on its own. When we scaffold instruction for ELLs, we support them as they become more independent in their learning.

Four types of scaffolding are especially effective for ELLs: (1) choosing appropriate materials; (2) simplifying the language; (3) providing models, guidelines, and choices so students don't have to generate everything themselves; and (4) using visuals and hands-on learning.

The building blocks below show examples of specific ways to scaffold instruction.

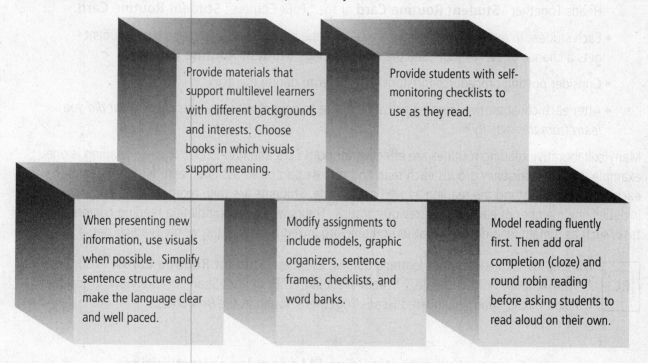

Provide materials that support multilevel learners with different backgrounds and interests. Choose books in which visuals support meaning.

Provide students with self-monitoring checklists to use as they read.

When presenting new information, use visuals when possible. Simplify sentence structure and make the language clear and well paced.

Modify assignments to include models, graphic organizers, sentence frames, checklists, and word banks.

Model reading fluently first. Then add oral completion (cloze) and round robin reading before asking students to read aloud on their own.

RC For other scaffolding activities, see "Step-Up Questioning," **Teacher Routine Card 1**; "Respond to Reading," **Teacher Routine Card 2**; "Language for Critical Thinking," **Teacher Routine Card 8**; and "Reading: Self-Monitoring Checklist," a **Student Routine Card**.

> ❝ **Scaffolding refers to providing contextual supports for meaning through the use of simplified language, teacher modeling, visuals and graphics, cooperative learning and hands-on learning.** ❞
>
> **—Ovando, Collier, & Combs (2003), p. 345**

ELL BEST PRACTICE ❻ Encourage Cooperative Learning

Encouraging cooperative learning is another way teachers can meet the unique needs of ELLs. Students learn from one another when they must collaborate and cooperate in order to complete a task or solve a problem. When ELLs participate in mixed-proficiency groups, all levels of language learners benefit. Cooperative learning also increases students' self-esteem.

Follow these tips when planning a cooperative learning activity:

- ELLs in particular will benefit from a clear structure for all cooperative learning activities. This includes providing clear procedures, sentence frames or other scaffolds for responding, and roles and responsibilities for each group member.

- The assignment should be at a level at which all students can be successful.

- Groups should be of approximately equal size. Ways to do this include using the "Numbered Heads Together" **Student Routine Card** or the "Four Corners" **Student Routine Card.**

- Each student in a group should have a role, and the roles should change so every student gets a chance at every "job." See the "Role-Taking" **Student Routine Card.**

- Consider posting procedures for students to refer to during the activity.

- After each collaborative learning activity, be sure to debrief with students. Ask: *What did you learn from this activity?*

Many collaborative reading routines are effective for both ELLs and non-ELLs. "Jigsaw" reading is one example. Mixed-proficiency groups each read and discuss part of an assigned text, with the goal of having each student understand the reading as well as possible. Students are then regrouped, so each new group includes one member of each of the previous groups. The new groups complete a reading comprehension task, such as a main idea/details (or other) graphic organizer, based on the whole reading passage.

 For step-by-step cooperative learning guides, use these **Student Routine Cards:** "Four Corners," "Write Around," "Roundtable," "Team Webbing," "Think/Pair/Share," "Interview," "Inside-Outside Circle," and "Numbered Heads Together," found in the *Resources.*

> ❝ **Cooperative activities give ELLs regular opportunities to discuss the content and to use the language of the school in a safe context…. In small cooperative groups, they can learn from their friends and classmates.** ❞
>
> —**Margarita Calderón et al. (2011), p. 113**

ELL BEST PRACTICE ❼　Draw from Student Experiences and Culture

Celebrating and drawing upon students' heritage cultures can enrich every classroom. Students who speak a language other than English bring knowledge and experience that expand everyone's horizons. In addition, asking your ELLs to share their primary language and their experiences accords them status as "experts." This helps your students build confidence and increases their motivation.

There are a variety of ways you can draw from student experiences and culture in your classroom:

- Research your ELLs' countries, cultures, history, and educational systems. Connect your lessons to something that the students already know.

- Choose books that are culturally relevant to your students. Ask questions about books and give writing prompts that ELLs can relate to: *Are any of the characters like people you know?*

- When teaching, ask ELLs to share what they know about the subject. You may be surprised to hear their answers!

- Find ways for your students to contribute their own cultural experiences to the classroom. Ask them how a topic or story connects to their lives or is the same or different in the culture of their family or heritage.

- Have a class multicultural day during which all students, ELLs and non-ELLs, are invited to share something about the history or background of their cultural heritage.

- Have all students, including ELLs, interview each other. Use the "Interview" **Student Routine Card** for this activity. Make sure to provide a list of questions and sentence frames to guide student responses: *Where are you from? How old are you? What languages do you speak? What is your favorite _____?*

For activities that draw from student experiences and culture, see "Cognates Choo-Choo Train," **Teacher Routine Card 7,** and the "Interview" **Student Routine Card,** found in the *Resources*.

> ❝ **Becoming familiar with the backgrounds and/or prior knowledge of ELL students allows a teacher to engage students in literacy experiences that connect with their diverse backgrounds, thereby building on this knowledge.** ❞
>
> —R. Cipriani-Sklar (2011), p. 14

ELL BEST PRACTICE ❽ Develop Academic Language and Critical Thinking

It is important for all ELLs to take part in activities that develop critical thinking skills. However, ELLs, like all students, need adequate background and vocabulary to support this type of thinking. Teaching students the academic language they need to understand and respond to higher-level questions will prepare them to be successful on standardized tests and at challenging assignments as they move up the grades. Perhaps most importantly, equipping students to discuss meaningful questions can help them see literature and language as important and meaningful topics.

In order to delineate academic language skills for critical thinking, we need to categorize thinking skills. There are at least five major areas in which all students need to develop higher-order thinking: comprehension, application, analysis, synthesis, and evaluation. The following are examples of useful verbs that teachers can use when asking questions in each area. You can teach ELLs the meaning of each of the verbs by providing specific models and examples of what to do when each of these words appears in class work, on homework, and on tests.

Academic Language for Critical Thinking

Comprehension: tell/describe; state/name; list; relate; explain; interpret; outline; discuss; distinguish; predict; restate; compare

Application: solve/complete; show/illustrate; use/construct; list; examine; classify

Analysis: analyze; distinguish; examine; explain; compare/contrast; investigate; identify; separate

Synthesis: create/invent; plan/compose; predict; construct/design; propose; imagine

Evaluation: select/choose; decide; justify/verify; debate/argue; recommend; assess; rate/prioritize

To extend opportunities for academic language development, provide sentence frames to support ELLs as they agree and disagree with their classmates' responses: *I agree with Miguel. I don't agree with Miguel because* _____. *My opinion is* _____.

RC	To develop academic language and critical thinking, see "Language for Critical Thinking," **Teacher Routine Card 8,** and "Teach Academic Language," **Teacher Routine Card 9.**

> ❝ **An important element of higher order thinking is learning to ask critical questions…. Teachers can begin this process by pre-teaching vocabulary and helping ELLs build background knowledge prior to reading.** ❞
>
> —Liz Fothergrill (2006), p. 1

ELL BEST PRACTICE ❾ Activate and Evaluate Background Knowledge

Before teaching a new subject, you have to first check whether your ELLs have the background knowledge to understand the new information they're going to learn. You do this by finding out what they already know; in other words, "activating background knowledge." After doing that, you have to evaluate their background knowledge against the prerequisite knowledge they need for the new topic and fill in any gaps you find.

This process is crucial for ELLs, because the development of and access to necessary background knowledge is essential for their comprehension of texts in English. Certain pieces of literature, such as stories about the early West or the American Revolution, will not make sense unless students understand the context in which the stories are set.

A "Do Now" is one easy way to activate and evaluate background knowledge before a lesson. Give a quick warm-up question or prompt, and have students write and/or draw their responses for you to evaluate. The prompt can be something as simple as *Draw a picture of a rain forest. Label parts of the picture.* With this information, you can determine who has the knowledge and who doesn't. Then you can group students for instruction.

Activating and Evaluating Background Knowledge

1. Determine what content students need to know. Provide students with a prompt.

2. Ask students to write a quick response. Give adequate time, but not too much.

3. Take a moment to review responses.

4. Use the information to create student groups and inform classroom instruction.

 For activities to help evaluate and activate background knowledge, see "Pop-Up," **Teacher Routine Card 6,** and "Exit Slips," **Teacher Routine Card 10,** found in the *Resources*.

> **❝ If a teacher has not activated prior knowledge or built background information about content material, teaching the vocabulary that is associated with the new content will not solve the problem. Just because ELLs may be able to read words doesn't mean they will understand their meaning in the context of the content being taught. ❞**
>
> —J. Haynes & D. Zacarian (2010), p. 24

ELL BEST PRACTICE ❿ Build In Ongoing Assessment

It is important to assess ELLs' progress on an ongoing basis. Traditional paper-and-pencil assessments, however, often test English language proficiency more than they test student learning. It is much more appropriate to assess ELLs based on their actual performance of classroom tasks. Because performance-based assessments do not require students to understand or use extensive language, they are particularly appropriate for ELLs.

Performance-based assessments evaluate what students have learned by observing them during a lesson. The assessments can include students creating products (writing samples, art projects, portfolios), doing a performance (oral reports, skits and plays, demonstrations), or process-oriented assessments (think-alouds, learning logs, self-assessment checklists).

Performance–Based Assessments for ELLs

Here are some tips for developing effective performance-based assessments for ELLs in your classroom.

- Provide meaningful, engaging tasks that are comprehensible to students.
- Use hands-on, collaborative activities.
- Assess during class time so it doesn't seem like a "test."
- Build into the task an informal assessment of language, both oral and written.
- Use a rubric to evaluate performance.
- Build in a form of self-assessment for students.
- Record results and keep a log of student progress over the year.

For activities to monitor performance, see "Respond to Reading," **Teacher Routine Card 2**; "Pick a Side," **Teacher Routine Card 3**; Pop-Up," **Teacher Routine Card 6**; "Exit Slips," **Teacher Routine Card 10**; and "Reading: Self-Monitoring Checklist," a **Student Routine Card,** all in the *Resources*.

> ❝... **Performance-based assessments can promote increased achievement for ELLs by increasing confidence in their ability to learn and motivation to continue learning.**❞
> —**Lorraine Valdez Pierce (2002), p. 3**

▶ Targeting Literacy Development

ELL-specific best practices are important, but sometimes good instruction for ELLs is very similar to good instruction for all students. This is particularly true in the case of literacy development. Like all students, ELLs in the reading classroom benefit from a focus on phonemic awareness, phonics, fluency, vocabulary, and comprehension. They also benefit from an increased emphasis on academic language and an appreciation of the role of their first language in literacy development. Following are strategies for targeting literacy development with ELLs in the reading classroom.

Academic Language Even if ELLs sound fully fluent when they speak, some may lack the academic language proficiency needed to read complex text and write informational and opinion pieces.

What to Do in the Classroom:

- Explicitly teach and practice academic vocabulary, including words that are especially difficult for ELLs (e.g., multiple-meaning words such as *table*, abstract words such as *each*).

- Rephrase unclear written statements, questions, and directions using simpler sentence structures (e.g., change passive voice to simple past tense; avoid embedded clauses).

- Explicitly teach and practice conjunctions that show logical relationships (e.g., *therefore, previously, although, such as*).

- Use **ELL Best Practices 1, 4, 5, 8, 9,** and **10**.

- Use **Teacher Routine Cards 1, 2, 3, 4, 6, 7, 8, 9,** and **10**.

Importance of First Language Whatever ELLs know in their primary language is helpful in learning to read and write in English.

What to Do in the Classroom:

- Help students discover similarities between their primary language and English. (See the Language Transfer Chart on pp. R81–R93.)

- Provide books in ELLs' primary language (especially books on topics students are learning about in English), and encourage students to read them.

- Allow students to use their primary language among themselves for tasks such as activating prior knowledge or planning writing.

- Use **ELL Best Practices 4, 5, 6, 7,** and **9**.

- Use **Teacher Routine Cards 7** and **9**.

Phonemic Awareness ELLs may need more time to develop sound-discrimination skills than students whose primary language is English.

What to Do in the Classroom:

- Use songs, poems, and chants to provide practice with auditory discrimination.

- Focus on sounds that don't exist in students' primary language or that are used differently (e.g., *b* and *v* are pronounced the same in Spanish). (See the Language Transfer Chart on pages R89–R92.)

- Use **ELL Best Practices 2, 3, 4, 7,** and **10.**

- Use **Teacher Routine Card 4.**

Phonics Phonics instruction should be connected to meaning to ensure that decoding instruction feels purposeful and meaningful.

What to Do in the Classroom:

- Use only words that students know the meaning of when teaching phonics.

- Make sure that decodable texts are comprehensible at the reader's proficiency level.

- Use **ELL Best Practices 1, 2, 3, 4,** and **10.**

- Use **Teacher Routine Card 4.**

Fluency Attaining grade-level fluency can be difficult for ELLs because their lack of proficiency in English may affect decoding, comprehension, and expression.

What to Do in the Classroom:

- Use group choral reading or reading along with the teacher to practice oral reading fluency.

- Use a familiar text that students have read several times before when practicing oral reading fluency.

- Use **ELL Best Practices 1, 3, 5, 6,** and **10.**

- Use **Teacher Routine Card 4.**

Vocabulary Supporting vocabulary development is one of the most important ways to improve comprehension skills in ELLs.

What to Do in the Classroom:

- Preteach vocabulary in a meaningful context (e.g., as part of a background-building activity, or as a preview of the text).

- Provide plenty of opportunities for students to practice and use vocabulary in different meaningful contexts.

- Use **ELL Best Practices 1, 2, 3, 4, 6, 7, 9,** and **10.**

- Use **Teacher Routine Cards 3, 4, 7,** and **9.**

> 66 **A small but consistent body of intervention research suggests that English learners will benefit most from rich, intensive vocabulary instruction that emphasizes 'student-friendly' definitions, that engages students in the meaningful use of word meanings in reading, writing, speaking, and listening, and that provides regular review.** 99
>
> —**Russell Gersten et al. (2007), p. 13**

Comprehension Building background knowledge can contribute greatly to improving ELLs' comprehension skills.

What to Do in the Classroom:

- Determine what information in a reading is crucial for comprehension, activate and evaluate students' background knowledge, and develop activities to fill gaps as necessary.

- Use primary language materials to help develop background knowledge when possible.

- Use hands-on and collaborative learning activities that require students to do something with the information provided in background building.

- Use **ELL Best Practices 2, 3, 6, 7, 9,** and **10.**

- All **Teacher Routine Cards** apply.

Assessment Considerations

▶ Ongoing Classroom Monitoring

Like their fluent English-speaking classmates, ELLs must demonstrate proficiency in reading and mathematics based on standardized tests. Assessment scores of fourth-grade ELLs on standardized reading assessments indicate a 36% achievement gap between these students and non-ELLs (National Assessment of Education Progress 2011). To help ensure success for ELLs, teachers must be able to accurately measure their progress throughout the school year so that the results can inform instruction.

Ongoing classroom monitoring may take many forms, from informal observations to written tests, and may include projects, oral presentations, or writing portfolios. This kind of ongoing monitoring informs instruction and helps teachers plan for intervention, create student work groups, and chart student progress.

When assessing ELLs, keep these general tips in mind:

- Make sure some of your assessments of ELLs are authentic and performance-based; that is, that they show students can do a specific task to demonstrate knowledge.

- Use a rubric and review it with students before the assignment so they know exactly what the expectations are.

- Give students the chance to assess themselves using the rubric.

- Monitor your students' progress using informal observation rubrics, such as the **ELL Progress Checkpoint Chart** provided on page 28.

- Take time to meet with students after assessments to recognize and acknowledge growth and to set future goals.

> **❝ As educators, we are constantly challenged to make informed decisions about our students; to do so, we plan, gather, and analyze information from multiple sources over time so the results are meaningful to teaching and learning. That's the core of the assessment process and the centerpiece in the education of linguistically and culturally diverse students. If reliable, valid, and fair for our students, assessment can be the bridge to educational equity. ❞**
>
> **—Margo Gottlieb (2006), p. 1**

ELLs and the Common Core State Standards

According to the Common Core State Standards Initiative, ELLs are expected to achieve the same high standards as students who speak English as their first language. The guidelines for applying the standards suggest that ELLs may need extra time, additional instructional support, and aligned assessments while they work to acquire both English language proficiency and content-area knowledge. (Common Core State Standards Initiative 2010)

▶ Modifying Existing Assessments for ELLs

To help your ELLs succeed on classroom tests, you can provide practical accommodations. It's also important to incorporate other forms of assessment to determine student progress. Simple strategies for doing this include:

- Give ELLs additional time to complete the test. This is the easiest of all accommodations.
- Allow a student translator to assist, especially during project assessments.
- Make use of comprehension supports, such as study buddies and cooperative groups.
- Incorporate alternative assessments, including project assessments and oral presentations.
- Adjust the "weighting" of curricular components (tests, homework, and classwork) to reflect student achievement.

Dialogue Journals

Dialogue journals are an excellent way to provide ongoing, personalized feedback to ELLs (and other students). They can also be a low-stress, high-interest tool for assessment, especially to assess reading and writing language objectives for ELLs. Long-term progress is easily assessed, since dialogue journals are a permanent and ongoing record of language skills.

- Dialogue journals can be print or electronic, and students should sit regularly to read the teacher's entry and write a short reply.
- Topics can be student or teacher generated and not limited to the curriculum.
- Teacher entries should relate to content/ideas expressed and language used and can include questions, suggestions, and encouragement.
- The language of teacher entries should match or go slightly beyond the language of a student's proficiency level.
- Teachers can use their entries to model correct language and use student entries to identify skills to be taught during class.

▶ Using a Checkpoint Chart

Use the ELL Progress Checkpoint Chart on the following page to chart your ELLs' growth. Throughout the year, record anecdotal evidence of each student's progress in listening, speaking, reading, and writing. Include notes on evidence of increasing comprehension, new words or phrases spoken, increases in reading fluency, and facility and correctness in writing.

You can also record social observations, such as increasing interaction with peers and willingness to speak up in class. Use this chart to make note of interventions used and any follow-up required.

ELL Progress Checkpoint Chart

Student _____   English Proficiency Level _____

Listening

Fall:

Winter:

Spring:

Speaking

Fall:

Winter:

Spring:

Reading

Fall:

Winter:

Spring:

Writing

Fall:

Winter:

Spring:

Social Observations

Interventions Used

Follow-Up Required

Notes

▶ Reading Assessments

Reading comprehension is an essential skill and one that is emphasized on standardized tests. You can assess your students' comprehension and fluency at the same time during normal reading instruction. By doing this periodically with your ELLs, you will be able to get a baseline to gauge growth, to intervene if necessary, and to predict students' readiness for standardized reading assessments.

Here are some important factors to consider as you plan and implement reading assessments:

- Be sure to select texts that are appropriate for individual students' grades and language proficiency levels.

- After ELLs have read a text aloud for fluency, let them read it again silently before checking their comprehension. Check comprehension by asking a few questions about the reading, or having students retell or summarize what they read.

- Try to informally assess your ELLs as they respond to questions during regular class time, so the results are authentic.

- Remember that an ELL's accent does not necessarily signal a lack of English fluency.

Once a reading assessment is complete, you can use the information you have collected to modify instruction. Students who are below proficient in any of the areas on the rubric may benefit from these teaching strategies that scaffold reading instruction:

1. Preteach any vocabulary that students will need to understand text. Use "Teach Academic Vocabulary," **Teacher Routine Card 9,** found in the *Resources*.

2. Check ELLs' background knowledge prior to reading.

3. Model reading fluently. This can be done by the teacher or by other students who are proficient in English and read fluently.

4. Expose students to multiple readings of the same text. Include choral reading, oral cloze, or round robin reading.

5. Have students read the text independently, either aloud or silently.

6. Regularly check for comprehension. You can ask suitable comprehension questions, have students retell what they have read, or have them complete a graphic organizer.

7. Encourage students to use the "Reading: Self-Monitoring Checklist" **Student Routine Card** (found in the *Resources*) as they read.

▶ Writing Assessments

Most teachers are familiar with the writing process. However, for those with ELLs in their classes, additional steps and time will need to be added, especially to prepare ELLs for writing assessments.

The typical writing process includes these steps:

1. Read the prompt.
2. Brainstorm a response.
3. Prewrite.
4. Write a first draft.

5. Confer with teacher or perhaps peers.
6. Revise.
7. Submit a final draft.

While this seems like a simple and straightforward process, ELLs will need additional support. When preparing ELLs for a writing assessment, try using the strategies below:

> **Sample prompt:** *Think about a tradition that is important to you. Write a story about the tradition. Give enough details for readers to understand why it's important to you.*

1. Have the students read the writing prompt twice. Do a "think-aloud" to restate what the prompt is asking (e.g., *First, I have to think about a tradition. What's a tradition? A tradition is a custom, or something people do a lot. What kind of tradition do I need to think about? A tradition that is important to me. Then I have to write a story about that tradition. The story should include details, or facts. Readers have to understand why that tradition is important to me.*).

2. When brainstorming a response, teach students how to restate the prompt to make a topic sentence (e.g., *One tradition that is important to me is _____*).

3. Show students how to prewrite using the **House Graphic Organizer** found in the *Resources*.

4. As ELLs write their first drafts, give support by reviewing language structures for explaining a sequence of events or for giving a main idea and supporting details. Provide students with sentence frames if they are struggling to write complete paragraphs.

5. There will be no peer editing during tests, but students can use the appropriate **Peer Conference Form**, found in the *Resources*, to practice finding errors.

6. Have students revise their writing, but explain that they may not have time to revise heavily during a test.

7. Review the final work against the scoring rubric that will be used for assessment. For tips and suggested responses to use during conferences, see **Writing: Student-Teacher Conferences** in the *Resources* section. You may also wish to use a **Writing Portfolio Growth Record,** also found in the *Resources,* to track student progress.

▶ Test–Taking Tips for ELLs

ELLs need to be prepared for important standardized tests, as well as everyday assessment in the classroom. Below are some tips and strategies for getting your ELLs ready for test success.

General Test–Taking Tips:

- Go through the test beforehand and highlight important key terms and phrases.
- Model how to look for cue words in the directions to know what is being asked.
- Remind students to answer the easy questions first, and go back to the difficult ones later.
- Review reading strategies students can use, such as checking for cognates or identifying literal vs. figurative language.
- Review and teach test-taking vocabulary. ELLs may not know the test-taking meaning of terms such as *explain*, *name*, *why?*, *how?*, *role of*, *discuss*, *think about*, *compare and contrast*, *define*, *describe briefly*, or *except*. Give them examples of questions and responses from other students' previous tests or from last year's tests.
- Teach students to use a bilingual dictionary. Some states allow ELLs to use them during tests.

For Multiple Choice/Fill in the Blank Questions, show ELLs how to

- practice putting each answer in the blank and reading the whole sentence silently.
- justify their answer by finding the evidence in the text.
- make an educated guess by crossing out the incorrect answers.

For Short Response Questions, model

- reviewing the questions before reading.
- numbering each paragraph to avoid having to go back and count paragraphs.
- how to restate the question as a statement.

For Essay Questions, remember to

- teach students the writing process.
- show student models of exemplary responses. (Student models of various genres at different proficiency levels can be found in the **Student Writing** section of the *Resources*.)
- review the scoring rubric that will be used for assessment so students will know what is expected of them.

Resources

Teacher Routine Cards

Use these routines regularly to help your ELLs be active participants in learning as they become proficient in English.

Student Routine Cards

Distribute Student Routine Cards as step-by-step guides for ELLs to use during activities.

Primary Grades

Intermediate Grades

Step-Up Questioning

Use multiple levels of language to help all ELLs respond to meaningful questions.

- For beginning ELLs, use questions with very simple vocabulary and grammar, so students can answer nonverbally or with single words.

- For low intermediate ELLs, use *who*, *what*, *when*, and *where* questions that can be answered using short phrases.

- For high intermediate ELLs, add *why* and *how* questions. Have students answer in complete sentences, but expect some grammatical errors.

- For proficient ELLs, use the same types of questions you would ask fluent English speakers, but expect minor errors.

Follow these steps:

1. Show pictures from a class reading selection.

2. Display a simple sentence about each picture.

   - For example, *Carlos is running*.

   - Act out the sentence.

   - Have students read the sentence with you.

3. Ask beginning students questions such as:

   - *Yes/no* questions: *Is Carlos walking?*

   - Option questions: *Who is running, Alex or Carlos?*

4. Ask low intermediate students questions such as:

   - Simple answer questions: *Where is Carlos running?*

   - Provide sentence frames and word banks, if necessary.

5. Ask high intermediate students questions such as:

   - *Why* questions: *Why is Carlos running?*

   - *How* questions: *How is Carlos running?*

6. Ask proficient ELLs the same kinds of questions you would ask non-ELLs.

Respond to Reading

This activity encourages ELLs to respond to reading through small group discussions and writing activities.

Follow these steps:

1. Do this activity after students have read a story or informational text.

2. Students will respond to questions at multiple proficiency levels. **Teacher Routine Card 1** has suggestions for questions at each language proficiency level.

3. Using one question at a time, have small groups of students discuss a question and brainstorm responses. Provide sentence frames and word banks for beginning and low intermediate students.

4. Encourage students to take notes while discussing each question.

5. After the discussion has ended, have students draft a written response.

6. Continue until each group has a written response for every question.

7. Encourage groups to share their work when finished.

Pick a Side

This activity helps students practice speaking and listening skills. It is useful for practicing new vocabulary or reviewing a class reading.

Follow these steps:

1. Use painters' tape to make a line through the middle of the classroom.

2. Instruct students to stand up at the front of the class.

3. Ask students questions such as these:

- *Which is better for your health, carrots or a soda?* (beginning level)

- *If you had a choice, would you rather live in a desert or a jungle?* (low intermediate level)

- *Do you think students should run or swim for exercise?* (high intermediate level)

4. As you ask the questions, point to the left side of the classroom for the first choice, and the right side for the second choice.

5. Instruct students to move to one side of the classroom or the other to answer the question.

6. Call on student volunteers to explain their answers. Provide sentence frames.

- *I chose _____ because I like _____.*

- *I prefer _____ because I do not like _____.*

7. Do not correct students' grammar as they speak. Rather, model correct usage as you respond to each student's answer.

Review Content and Language Objectives

This simple routine will help make students responsible for their learning every day.

Follow these steps:

1. Plan content and language objectives for your lessons with this graphic organizer.

What *content* do I want my students to learn? (goal/objective) Students will be able to:	What *language* do my students need to know to meet this objective? Students will be able to:
What will the students need to do to learn this content? (activities)	What will the students need to do to learn this language? (activities)
How will I know if students have mastered the content? (assessment)	How will I know if students have mastered the language? (assessment)
What will I do to reteach the content, if necessary? (additional activities)	What will I do to reteach the language, if necessary? (additional activities)

2. Write the objectives on the board in simple, comprehensible language.

3. Before teaching, review the objectives with students.

4. Assign a daily "ambassador" from among your ELLs.

- The ambassador will tell classroom visitors what the objectives are.

- This reinforces the objectives and helps students practice their speaking skills.

5. After each lesson, review the objectives.

6. Ask students if the lesson objectives were met.

- If not, discuss why not.

- Also discuss what could be changed to help students meet the objectives.

Modified Total Physical Response (TPR)

Students learn by doing. Total Physical Response (TPR) is a movement-based language-learning strategy in which the teacher says commands appropriate to the students' English language proficiency levels. Students respond by following the commands, which develops ELLs' listening skills and reinforces the meanings of the vocabulary words.

As students learn more English, you can make the commands more difficult by giving multiple-step commands using embedded clauses (*Pick up the book that is on Ana's desk, and put it on the teacher's desk.*) or using hypothetical language (*If Juan is wearing blue jeans, raise your hand.*). As students gain confidence in English, they can also take turns giving the commands.

The activity below is a variation of TPR that can be used with commands that relate to a reading selection.

Follow these steps:

1. Write commands at appropriate proficiency levels on strips of paper, one for each student. Example commands:

   • *Point to Sarah.* (Beginning)

   • *Point to the main character.* (Low intermediate)

   • *Show me what Sarah did at the end of the book. Now tell me: What did she do?* (High intermediate)

   • *If Sarah was happy at the end of the book, stand up. If she was not happy, raise your hand and tell me why.* (Proficient)

2. Have students take turns reading their commands.

3. The rest of the class should respond to each command.

   • Beginning ELLs may not be able to respond to all commands.

   • Encourage beginners to listen to the command and do what other students do.

Pop-Up

In a Pop-up activity, students each take turns standing up, giving their answer, and then sitting down again, in quick succession. Pop-up is a great way to get ELLs to hone their listening skills and practice responding orally to simple questions. Pop-ups can also serve as informal assessments during and after reading or as a way to evaluate students' background knowledge of a subject.

Follow these steps:

1. Ask volunteers to model the activity by doing these things in quick succession:

- Stand up.

- Say their full name and age.

- Sit down again.

2. Ask students a question. For example:

- *Name one cause for the Civil War that we read about in this book.*

- *What is another word for _____?*

- *What do you think the character's conflict is?*

3. Provide a word bank on the board.

- Beginning students may find it difficult to come up with words quickly.

- Encourage them to find and say a one-word answer from the word bank.

4. Do not correct individual student's responses as they answer. Instead, model correct usage, and make notes for later review and practice.

5. When all students have responded, review and discuss the correct answer(s).

- Use sentence frames to structure discussion.

- For example: *I agree* or *I disagree because _____.*

Cognates Choo-Choo Train

This activity will help your Spanish-speaking ELLs gain confidence as they learn words that are similar in English and Spanish. Students who do not know Spanish will learn new words, too!

Follow these steps:

1. Designate a Cognates Wall and label it accordingly.

2. Decorate the wall with colorful paper, with a train track snaking around the border.

3. Use index cards to resemble cars on a train.

4. Review some of the English/Spanish cognates on pages R79–R80.

5. Tell students to look for cognates in their reading.

- Have them add a car to the train when they find a cognate.

- Students can illustrate the word and/or write the meaning on the card.

6. Encourage all students to look for cognates everywhere.

7. Be mindful of false cognates (e.g., *library/librería*, which means *bookstore* in Spanish).

8. Once a month, review and celebrate the new words students have learned.

Language for Critical Thinking

Directions:

Use prompts like the ones below to encourage students (both ELLs and non-ELLs) to think critically about texts they read. Provide models and sentence frames to guide all student responses. Allow beginning ELLs to answer with one-word responses.

	Beginning	Low and High Intermediate	Proficient
Comprehend	Name the characters in this story.	Describe your favorite character.	Compare and contrast two characters.
Apply	Draw a picture that shows what this text is about.	Explain how this text is an example of _____.	Use what you learned to construct/describe your own _____.
Analyze	Tell what words this author uses to show _____.	Identify the purpose of this text.	Explain how the ideas in this text are organized.
Synthesize	Tell what is the same in these three texts.	Draw a chart that shows how the main ideas in this text are connected.	Imagine and describe a different conclusion for this text.
Evaluate	Pick a good text for someone else. Why is it good?	Describe these texts and choose the best one.	Rate this text by discussing its strengths and weaknesses.

Teach Academic Vocabulary

Teach an academic vocabulary word each day. Use this routine every time you teach a new word. You can use this routine with all your students.

Follow these steps:

1. Identify the new word and write it on the board.

2. Say the word aloud and have students repeat the word several times.

3. Have students give a thumbs-up if they know the meaning of the word. If they're not sure of the meaning, have them give a thumbs-down.

4. Explain the meaning of the word.

- Write a student-friendly explanation on the board.

- Give examples.

- If applicable, provide a Spanish cognate.

5. Have students write the word and the meaning in their notebooks.

6. Give each student a piece of paper, folded into quarters.

7. Have students make a Four Corners chart for each word:

- Write the word in one section of the paper.

- Write the meaning in another section.

- Write a sentence using the word in the third section.

- Draw a picture in the fourth section.

8. Discuss the pictures the students have drawn. *How does the picture represent the word?*

9. Display sample Four Corners charts in the classroom. Review all new words weekly.

Exit Slips

An Exit Slip is an easy, informal way to check understanding after a lesson. It is also a way to evaluate students' background knowledge when preparing to teach a new lesson.

NOTE: All students will be answering the same question in this activity. To support students at lower English proficiency levels, pair them with more proficient students.

Follow these steps:

1. Just before the end of the day (or end of the class), give each student a piece of scrap paper or a self-stick note.

2. Have students write their names and the date on the paper.

3. Reveal the question/statement of the day; read it aloud. For example:

- *Summarize what you learned today, using one or two sentences.*

- *What is an example of _____?*

- *What is another word for _____?*

- *List one fact about _____.*

4. Ask students to write their responses on their papers. Have intermediate and proficient ELLs use complete sentences.

5. Collect papers as students leave the class.

6. Review student responses and make two piles.

- One pile is for students who do not need additional assistance.

- One pile is for those who do.

7. Meet with the students who need additional help and preteach or reteach, as necessary.

Name _____

Four Corners

Follow the steps:

1. Choose a topic.

2. Join a group.

3. Talk.

4. Share.

To the Teacher: Assign one topic to each of four areas of the room. Each child should choose a topic, go to that area, and discuss the topic with the other children in that area. Model the activity, and circulate as children choose their topics and areas. Remind them that everyone in the group must talk. After a short time, call on one child to share what the group talked about. Allow children to use gestures and pictures to make their meaning clear.

Name _____

Write-Around

Follow the steps:

1. Listen to the question.

2. Take turns.
   Write answers.

3. Share.

To the Teacher: Organize children in small groups, and tell them you will ask a question and they will take turns writing an answer. Make sure each group has a sheet of paper and at least one pencil. Provide a word bank or sentence frames for children to refer to during the activity. Ask the question, using visuals and gestures to support understanding. Then have children take turns, each writing an answer. Allow children who have trouble to ask for help or draw a picture. Then call on one child to share the group's answers.

Name _____

Roundtable

Follow the steps:

1. Listen to the question.

2. Take turns.
   Answer the question.

3. Listen to the other answers.

4. Share.

To the Teacher: Organize children in small groups, and tell them you will ask a question and each group member must say an answer. Remind children to listen to each other's answers. Ask the question, using visuals and gestures to support understanding. Provide sentence frames or a word bank for children. Then have children take turns, each saying an answer. Allow children who have trouble to ask for help or draw a picture. Then call on one child to share the group's answers.

Name _____

Team Webbing

Follow the steps:

1. Listen to the question.

2. Write in the web.

3. Pass the paper.

4. Write again.

5. Share.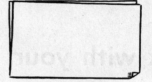

To the Teacher: Model this activity for children first. Organize them in small groups, and tell them you will ask a question and they will take turns writing an answer. Make sure each group has a sheet of paper and each child has a pencil. Ask the question, using visuals and gestures to support understanding. Provide sentence frames and word banks for children. Then have children take turns, each writing an answer. Allow children who have trouble to ask for help or draw a picture. Then call on one child to share the group's answers.

Name _____

Think / Pair / Share

Follow the steps:

1. Listen.

2. Think on your own.

3. Talk with your partner.

4. Share.

To the Teacher: Allow children sufficient time to think before having them discuss the topic or question in pairs. Encourage children to write their thoughts during this time. For sharing, you may want to encourage both children in turn to say something about what they discussed. Allow children to use gestures and pictures to make their meaning clear.

Name _____

Interview

Follow the steps:

1. Ask questions.

2. Listen.

3. Answer questions.

4. Share.

To the Teacher: Organize children into pairs, and have them take turns asking each other questions. Provide sample sentences and responses for children to refer to during the interview. Encourage listeners to take notes or draw pictures to help them remember their partners' answers. Then call on children to tell what their partners said.

Inside-Outside Circle

Follow the steps:

1. Some children will be inside.

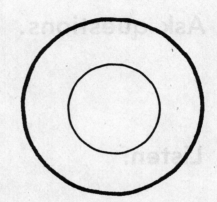

2. Some children will be outside.

3. Talk with your partner.

4. Move.

To the Teacher: Organize children into an inner circle and an outer circle, with each child facing a partner. Then have partners discuss a question or practice a language skill until you tell them to stop and move to the next partner. You can also have children switch circles with their partners.

Name _____

Four Corners

Follow the steps:

1. Look at the four topics your teacher will list.

2. Choose one topic.

3. Go to the part of the room where your topic will be discussed.

4. Talk about your topic. Your teacher will tell you when to stop.

5. One group member will "report out."
   ➤**TIP** When your teacher asks you, tell about what your group talked about. Say as much as you can. If you can't think of a word, use the word bank or ask another group member for help.

6. When other groups report out, listen.
   ➤**TIP** Take notes and draw pictures to help you remember.

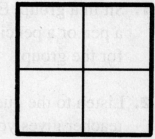

To the Teacher: Before asking students to complete the activity independently, explicitly explain each step and check for understanding. Model the steps with more-proficient students. Provide a word bank for students to use if needed. Distribute these directions as a reminder of the steps to follow, and circulate to monitor participation and understanding.

Write-Around

Follow the steps:

1. Sit in a group. Each person should have a pen or a pencil. Use one sheet of paper for the group.

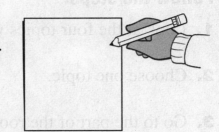

2. Listen to the question or prompt your teacher gives you. You will have two minutes.

3. The first person writes an answer. Then he or she passes the paper to the next person.

4. Each group member must write one answer.

   ➤**TIP** If you cannot think of what words to use, you may ask another student for help. You may also draw a picture.

5. Your teacher will tell you when to stop working.

6. When your teacher asks you, tell about your group's answers.

   ➤**TIP** Say as much as you can. It is okay if you cannot tell about all the answers.

To the Teacher: Before asking students to complete the activity independently, explicitly explain each step and check for understanding. Distribute these directions as a reminder of the steps to follow, and circulate to monitor participation and understanding.

Name _____

Roundtable

Follow the steps:

1. Sit in a group.

2. Listen to the question or the prompt your teacher gives you.

3. Take turns. Each group member must give at least one answer.

4. When it is your turn, speak.
   ➤**TIP** If you cannot think of a word, you may ask another student for help. You may also draw a picture.

5. When it is not your turn, listen.
   ➤**TIP** Take notes and draw pictures to help you remember.

6. Your teacher will tell you when to stop working.

7. When your teacher calls on you, tell about your group's answers.

To the Teacher: Before asking students to complete the activity independently, explicitly explain each step and check for understanding. Model the steps with more-proficient students. Distribute these directions as a reminder of the steps to follow, and circulate to monitor participation and understanding.

Team Webbing

Follow the steps:

1. Sit in a group. Use a large sheet of paper.

2. Listen to the topic your teacher gives you.

3. Draw a big web.

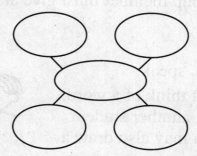

4. Write in the part of the web that is near you. Leave room for other group members to write in the same space.

➤**TIP** If you cannot think of which words to use, ask another student for help, use the word bank, or draw a picture.

5. When your teacher tells you, turn the web. A new part of the web will be in front of each person.

6. Write in the part of the web that is near you now. Your teacher will tell you when to stop.

7. When your teacher calls on you, tell about what you and your group wrote.

To the Teacher: Before asking students to complete the activity independently, explicitly explain each step and check for understanding. Model the steps with more-proficient students. Provide a word bank for students to choose from. Distribute these directions as a reminder of the steps to follow, and circulate to monitor participation and understanding.

Name _____

Think/Pair/Share

Follow the steps:

1. Listen to the question or the prompt your teacher gives you.

2. THINK: Think by yourself.

3. PAIR: Meet with your partner. Talk about your ideas. Your teacher will tell you when to stop.
   ➤**TIP** You can take notes to help you remember.

4. SHARE: When your teacher calls on you, tell what you and your partner talked about.

To the Teacher: Before asking students to complete the activity independently, explicitly explain each step and check for understanding. Model the steps with a more-proficient student. Distribute these directions as a reminder of the steps to follow, and circulate to monitor participation and understanding.

Name _____

Interview

Follow the steps:

1. Sit with a partner.

2. Listen to the question or the prompt your teacher gives you.

3. Ask your partner a question.

4. Your partner will answer.

5. When your teacher tells you, switch. Your partner will ask you a question.

6. You will answer. Keep on asking and answering questions. Your teacher will tell you when to stop.

7. When your teacher calls on you, tell about your partner's answers.
   ➤**TIP** Say as much as you can.

To the Teacher: Before asking students to complete the activity independently, explicitly explain each step and check for understanding. Model the steps with a more-proficient student. Provide sample questions and answers for students to refer to. Distribute these directions as a reminder of the steps to follow, and circulate to monitor participation and understanding.

Name _____

Student Routine Cards
ELL TEACHER'S HANDBOOK

Intermediate Grades

Inside-Outside Circle

Follow the steps:

1. One group stands in the inside circle.

2. One group stands in the outside circle.

3. Listen to the question or the prompt.

4. Students in the outside circle will say something.

> ➤**TIP** If you cannot think of which words to use, you may use movements or point to a picture. You may also ask your partner or use the sentence frames or word bank for help.

5. Students in the inside circle will say something.

6. Your teacher will tell you when to switch places or move.

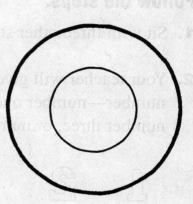

To the Teacher: Before asking students to complete the activity independently, explicitly explain each step and check for understanding. Provide sentence frames or word banks for students to use as needed. After the first prompt, you may want to have one circle rotate one person to the right so that students have different partners for the next prompt. You may also have students in the inside circle trade places with students in the outside circle. Distribute these directions as a reminder of steps to follow, and circulate to monitor participation and understanding.

Numbered Heads Together

Follow the steps:

1. Sit with three other students.

2. Your teacher will give each person a number—number one, number two, number three, or number four.

1   2   3   4

3. Listen to the topic your teacher gives you.

4. Talk about the topic with your group.

➤**TIP** Every group member should talk. Take turns.

5. Make sure each person can say at least one thing about the topic.

➤**TIP** Practice saying one thing.

6. Your teacher will tell you when to stop.

7. When your teacher calls your number, say at least one thing you talked about.

To the Teacher: Before asking students to complete a group activity independently, explicitly explain each step and check for understanding. Model the steps with two more-proficient students. Provide sentence starters if necessary. Distribute these directions as a reminder of the steps to follow, and circulate to monitor participation and understanding. Use this activity with the "Role-Taking" routine on page R27.

Role-Taking

Follow the steps:

1. Sit in a group.

2. Each person will have one role, or job. Here are some jobs:
- Reader
- Writer
- Reporter
- Timekeeper

3. Listen to the question or the prompt your teacher gives you.

4. Work together on the question or prompt. Your teacher will tell you when to stop.

5. If you are the Reader, read aloud to your group.
➤**TIP** Read slowly. Stop and make sure everyone understands.

6. If you are the Writer, write about what the group says.

7. If you are the Reporter, you will share your group's work.

8. If you are the Timekeeper, you will keep your group on schedule.

To the Teacher: Before asking students to complete the activity independently, explicitly explain each step and check for understanding. If you assign different roles, make sure students understand their jobs by modeling each role. Remind students that every group member must contribute. Distribute these directions as a reminder of the steps to follow, and circulate to monitor participation and understanding.

Reading: Self-Monitoring Checklist

Follow these steps as you read:

1. LOOK: Look at the title, pictures, and captions.

2. PREDICT: Make predictions about the text. Write your predictions in your reading journal.

3. LIST: Make a list of words you don't know in your reading journal.

4. WRITE: Ask questions while you read. Write these questions in your journal.

5. SUMMARIZE: Using your own words, describe what you read about.

To the Teacher: Model the activity with students before implementing it. Think aloud as you walk through each of the steps, reviewing and teaching vocabulary as needed (e.g., *captions*, *predictions*). Provide a reading journal for students to log their reading and record their predictions, new vocabulary, questions, and summaries. Encourage students to draw pictures. Review work with students and give them feedback in their reading journals.

Name _____

Writing: House Graphic Organizer

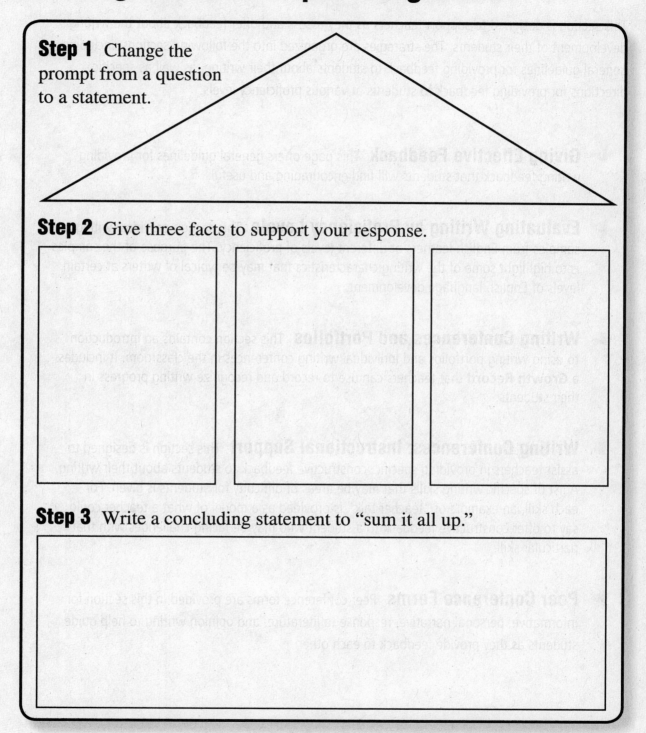

Step 1 Change the prompt from a question to a statement.

Step 2 Give three facts to support your response.

Step 3 Write a concluding statement to "sum it all up."

To the Teacher: Remind students that writing an essay is like building a house. You need a strong foundation, a roof, and supports (use visuals to demonstrate the meanings of these terms as necessary). Have students practice creating this graphic organizer on their own to help keep their ideas and writing organized.

Responding to Student Writing

Overview

This section is designed to support teachers as they assess and offer feedback about the writing development of their students. The strategies are organized into the following sections, including general guidelines for providing feedback to students about their writing, as well as specific directions for providing feedback to students at various proficiency levels.

▶ **Giving Effective Feedback** This page offers general guidelines for providing writing feedback that students will find encouraging and useful.

▶ **Evaluating Writing by Proficiency Levels** This section provides writing samples from English learners at different levels of proficiency. The purpose of the samples is to highlight some of the writing characteristics that may be typical of writers at certain levels of English language development.

▶ **Writing Conferences and Portfolios** This section contains an introduction to using writing portfolios and individual writing conferences in the classroom. It includes a **Growth Record** that teachers can use to record and recognize writing progress in their students.

▶ **Writing Conferences: Instructional Support** This section is designed to assist teachers in providing specific, constructive feedback to students about their writing. A list of specific writing skills that may be areas of difficulty for students is given. For each skill, an example of "teacher talk" is provided as a model of what a teacher could say to offer constructive feedback to a student who may be facing challenges with that particular skill.

▶ **Peer Conference Forms** Peer conference forms are provided in this section for informative, personal narrative, response to literature, and opinion writing to help guide students as they provide feedback to each other.

Giving Effective Feedback

Effective feedback on students' writing has the following characteristics:

▶ **Effective instructional feedback is clear and consistent.**
Be sure to use language that a student can understand when giving feedback.
If students do not understand what to correct, they will not be able to improve.
Also, provide the same type of feedback each time you confer with students.

▶ **Effective instructional feedback is seen as useful by students.** Instructional feedback should help students develop a positive attitude toward correcting errors in their writing. Students should understand that correcting errors in their writing will help them to better convey their intended message to the reader.

▶ **Effective instructional feedback is supplemented with instruction.** To help students improve their future writing, provide explicit instruction and sufficient practice in using the skills targeted in the instructional feedback.

▶ **Effective instructional feedback provides students with information on their strengths as well as areas of concern.**
The types of errors that students make in their writing are just one indication of their writing proficiency. The ways in which a student uses the English language correctly and effectively are also indicators of proficiency. When providing feedback, focus on a student's strengths in using the English language as well as on areas that need improvement.

▶ **Effective instructional feedback is encouraging, not discouraging.** Feedback should help students improve their use of English, not discourage them from writing. Feedback should be phrased in a positive way in order to encourage students to grow and stretch as writers.

Providing feedback on students' writing will help them in all their academic endeavors. For specific suggestions on how to provide instructional support to help students improve their writing, see pages R54–R57.

Evaluating Writing by Proficiency Levels

This section provides an overview of evaluating writing by proficiency levels for English language learners, spanning three levels of English-language proficiency: Beginning/Early Intermediate, Intermediate, and High Intermediate/Proficient.

Each student model is written in response to a prompt. Following each model is a list of characteristics commonly found in ELL writing samples at each proficiency level. Generally, teachers can expect the following in ELLs' writing:

Beginning/Early Intermediate ELLs should be able to

- Copy words and short phrases, progressing to writing phrases and short, simple sentences, but with many grammar and spelling errors

- Use invented spelling to write common words and short predictable phrases

- Use general vocabulary and high-frequency words.

Intermediate ELLs should be able to

- Write simple and expanded sentences with some grammatical errors

- Write more coherently but with little complexity

- Use some academic language and technical vocabulary.

High Intermediate/Proficient ELLs should be able to

- Write with a variety of sentence structures

- Write with clarity, good organization, and minimal errors

- Use academic and technical vocabulary.

Of course, every child is unique in his or her acquisition of the English language and will have different strengths and challenges as he or she develops as a writer. These samples are not comprehensive and are meant to give only a general overview of what a teacher might encounter.

Student Models and Explanations

Primary Grades

Student models from English learners are provided for three spans of English-language development proficiency: Beginning/Early Intermediate, Intermediate, and High Intermediate/Proficient. Each of the following student models is in response to the writing prompt below:

Writing a Personal Narrative

▶ **Write a story about a time when you learned something from a friend.**

When you write about this experience, remember to

- include a beginning, a middle, and an end;
- use details to describe the experience; and
- use correct grammar, spelling, punctuation, and capitalization.

Following each response is a list of characteristics to illustrate areas of strength and challenges often seen in the writing of children at that proficiency level.

Student Model

Beginning and Early Intermediate Proficiency Levels

How to ride a bike.
My friend who teach me. She
teach me how to hode the bike.
She teach me, and she push the
bike We take turn. and we have
lost of fun ler how to ride a bike.

Student Model Explanation

Beginning and Early Intermediate

This model is in response to the writing prompt given on page R33. The writing sample features characteristics that may be common for children at the Beginning and Early Intermediate stages of English language development.

General Characteristics

At the Beginning or Early Intermediate proficiency level, a child may

- progress from writing in simple words or phrases to writing in simple sentences with subjects and predicates.

- write in the simple present-tense or present progressive tense (*I walk, I am walking*).

- use common nouns and verbs.

- begin to use articles *a*, *an*, and *the*.

- begin to use some prepositions and conjunctions.

- begin to use descriptive adjectives.

Student Model
Intermediate Proficiency Level

My friends

My friends help me how
to do the homerk when I was
small because I dint now how to doit And I dint
now how to do swims when I was small to I was
two hers on I cilit wolk and I cip foling
in the floor And I dint now how to hich the
ball I wont to do the swims when I was
doing it then I feel down then my friend picks
me up, She Owes helps me how to do
evryone and she is nice to me She talk
me evrywear when I tell her
stvff I want her to

Student Model Explanation

Intermediate

This model is in response to the writing prompt given on page R33. The writing sample features characteristics that may be common for children at the Intermediate stage of English language development.

General Characteristics

At the Intermediate proficiency level, a child may

- begin to use both simple and compound sentences with some complex sentences.

- begin to use regular and irregular past and past progressive tense verbs (*have, has, had; do, does, did; was walking, were walking*) as well as some future tense verbs.

- use correct agreement between subject and predicate.

- begin to use comparative and descriptive adjectives.

- begin to use pronouns correctly.

- begin to use many prepositions and conjunctions correctly.

- begin to use the possessive *'s* and plurals ending with *-s* and *-es*.

Student Model
High Intermediate and Proficient Levels

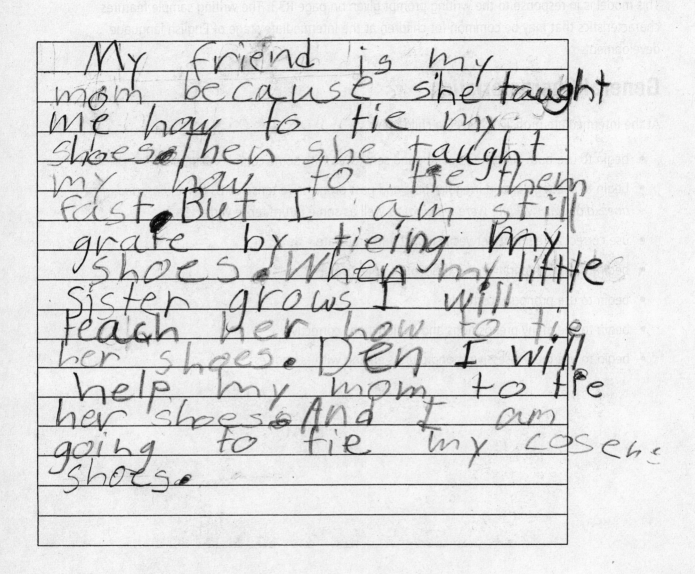

My friend is my mom because she taught me how to tie my shoes. then she taught my how to tie them fast. But I am still grate by tieing my shoes. When my little sister grows I will teach her how to tie her shoes. Den I will help my mom to tie her shoes. And I am going to tie my cosens shoes.

Student Model Explanation

High Intermediate and Proficient

This model is in response to the writing prompt given on page R33. The writing sample features characteristics that may be common for children at the High Intermediate and Proficient stages of English language development.

General Characteristics

At the High Intermediate or Proficient level, a child may

- use many compound and complex sentences.
- attempt to use more extensive vocabulary.
- sometimes use contractions, possessives, and plural forms correctly.
- use idioms and figures of speech.

Student Models and Explanations

Intermediate Grades

Student models from English learners are provided for three spans of English-language development proficiency: Beginning/Early Intermediate, Intermediate, and High Intermediate/Proficient. Each of the following student models is in response to the writing prompt below:

Writing a Narrative

▶ **Write a story about a person who learns to do something that was once hard for him or her.**

When you write this narrative, remember to

- include a beginning, a middle, and an end;

- use details to describe the experience; and

- use correct grammar, spelling, punctuation, and capitalization.

Following each writing sample is a list of characteristics to illustrate areas of strength and challenges often seen in the writing of students at that proficiency level.

Student Model
Beginning and Early Intermediate Proficiency Levels

Hai my name is _____, and I am
in 6th, I am 11 yer old. I am going
to tuoe you a story about a boy
name Jason and a boy name Jason.
    Jason is in 3th and Joson is in
3th too, dey are good farend.
onw-day Joson is sead becus he dot now how
to dow X taboe. but he is good at spelling,
and Jason is good at X taboe but, He
is not good at spelling, so we deside to
help earenor, like a time. First Jason
help Joson at Xtaboe so Jason tuy Joson
a trak. Joson tink is a little eizey so Jason
tuy him a nothe trak and Joson tink
is so eizey now. Joson tich Jason at
spelling tim so we work haerd but
Jason said spelling is so hard. Joson
said spelling is hard but is eizey too
so Joson to Jason same trik, Jason
said iedis eizey. so Jason wo and work
fanly Jason now how to rarit. 30 word
at 60 min.
    So Jason now how to do spelling
and Joson now how to do X taboe. In
school dey gat A+ on the teias.
Jason and Joson is so happly about
dear teias. so duy desid to work like
a time naxe time too. The end

Student Model Explanation

Beginning and Early Intermediate

This model is in response to the writing prompt given on page R40. The writing sample features characteristics that may be common for students at the Beginning and Early Intermediate stages of English language development.

General Characteristics

At the Beginning and Early Intermediate levels of proficiency, a student may

- progress from writing in single words or phrases to writing in simple sentences with a subject and predicate.

- write in the simple present tense or present progressive tense.

- begin to use past progressive tense.

- use correct agreement between subject and predicate.

- begin to use subject, object, and possessive pronouns.

- begin to use irregular verbs.

- advance to correct use of plurals ending with -s and -es.

- begin to use articles *a*, *an*, and *the*.

- begin to use locational and directional prepositions.

- begin to use conjunctions *and*, *or*, and *but*.

- begin to use descriptive adjectives.

Student Model
Intermediate Proficiency Level

Their met was a man named ——. He is my father, and he is a chinese. He is a good builder chief. He can lead Some builder to fix Something or making good apartment or house. The work has a little bit hard. But he can get more money for our family. He is 44 years old, and he has a wife —— that is my mom. she is 33 years old and she is a great nurse.

—— is a good Soccer player. when he is in the China, he is always play Soccer and very good at Soccer. But when he is come to US. The work is hard and he became old let him gotten bad at Soccer. right now he is always play Soccer too.

—— family has a lot of happy. He/has one son and Two Daughter. I'm his only son. And I have a sister name ——. I have a Yuger sister name ——. my sister —— is Seventeen years old.

She is very good to me and to to every body. my yuger sister —— is still not born. she is syuger then me 11 years.

—— is working very hard. He is very black by the Sun when he is building. right now our family has a lot of problem for —— to doing. So he is working hard and hard.

—— has a lot of white hair on his head. He is very loves me and I'm very love him, love my dad.

Student Model Explanation

Intermediate

This model is in response to the writing prompt given on page R40. The writing sample features characteristics that may be common for students at the Intermediate stage of English language development.

General Characteristics

At the Intermediate level of proficiency, a student may

- begin to use both simple and compound sentences with some complex sentences.

- begin to use many regular and irregular past tense verbs, as well as future tense verbs.

- begin to use comparative adjectives and multiple descriptive adjectives.

- begin to use possessive nouns.

- begin to use most possessive and object pronouns.

- begin to use many prepositions.

- begin to use both coordinating (e.g., *for, so*) and subordinating (e.g., *because, after, when*) conjunctions.

- begin to use positive and negative statements and questions.

- begin to use sentences that contain more detailed and specific vocabulary.

Student Model
High Intermediate and Proficient Levels

Beep Beep the alarm rang as Emma struggle to get out of bed. She loves to cook and wants to become a famouse chef. when she grows up. Emma has long brown hair and she is asian. Her parents are divorse but she is still living a wonderful life.

   One morning Emma went to pick up shopping supply, while walking she pass by a cooking contest flyer. She had a great idea, "Hey maybe I should enter" as a wonderful cook Emma is she still hesn't figure out her pass gramother chilly sauce recipy yet. She got home and ask her mother if she has the secret recipy that has been passed down through generation, her mom doesn't have a clue.

(continued on page R46)

(continued from page R45)

Emma worked and worked to make the most deliciouse chilly sauce, but all have faild. She took a rest and thinked hard. She wanted to try it another time to see if it worked. Failer...Emma put the pot there and she knocked over ground pepper and other ingredient in there. "Oh no" she said. She took a spoon and took a sip IT TAST DELICIOUSE!.

Next morning, she went to the cooking contest the Judge tasted the chilly she made and was surprise. She won and now is the most famouse chef in the whole united state. That is the story of a girl who once struggle with cooking and learn from her mistakes.

Student Model Explanation

High Intermediate and Proficient

This model is in response to the writing prompt given on page R40. The writing sample features characteristics that may be common for students at the High Intermediate and Proficient stages of English language development.

General Characteristics

At the High Intermediate and Proficient levels, a student may

- use many compound and complex sentences.

- attempt to use more extensive vocabulary.

- use conditional form (e.g., *If....then*).

- use indefinite pronouns (e.g., *anyone, everything*).

- use many idioms and figures of speech.

Peer Editing

Overview

Using peer editing with ELLs helps them build English speaking and listening skills as they interact with other students. Peer editing also helps students build self-confidence as they become more proficient in the evaluation and editing process. Finally, with peer editing, ELLs improve their own writing as they learn what to look for in skillful examples.

Many teachers hesitate to use peer editing with ELLs or any students with lower-level writing skills. However, by modeling the activity and providing plenty of practice, the peer editing routine can be successful with all students.

Steps for Peer Editing

1. Model the activity with students first. Focus on a single different item from the rubric each time you model.

- Project a student model and allow time for students to read it.

- Give each student a copy of the rubric.

- Use a think-aloud to identify an example from the model that needs improvement and to give feedback to the writer.

- Have a pair of students model identifying and giving feedback using another student model.

2. Assign partners for peer editing.

- Sometimes partner ELLs with other students at the same English language proficiency level; ELLs will not be able to edit writing that is beyond their language level. On other occasions, partner ELLs of mixed proficiencies to allow them to mentor and learn from each other.

- Pair ELLs from the same language background whenever possible, to allow them to give more detailed feedback in their first language.

- Have pairs focus on a single item from the rubric when they work together.

3. Make sure students have first drafts of their assignments ready before they pair up.

4. Remind students to read their partner's draft at least twice: once for overall flow and organization, and again to identify examples of the focus item.

5. Monitor students for fairness and respect as they give feedback. If time allows, they may give feedback on items other than the focus item.

6. Have dictionaries and thesauruses on hand (as appropriate for the focus item). Model using these resources, as necessary.

Writing: Student–Teacher Conferences

Overview

Teachers often feel they don't have enough time in the day to hold individual writing conferences, but conferencing is essential, especially for ELLs. A conference helps students by giving them one-on-one time with their teacher. During that time, teachers can give students feedback on writing strengths, as well as track and review writing growth.

Tips for Talking About Writing

1. Decide which students you will conference with on a specific day and how long you'll spend with each student.

2. Decide what activity the other students will be doing. (The activity should be at a normal level of noise for your class, so students in the writing conference will feel more comfortable.)

3. You may want to have students self-assess their work before they come to you. When you meet, ask them what they thought they did well in the writing.

4. Focus on strengths, but try to mention one writing challenge between two strengths. For example: *I like the way you begin. It grabs my attention. Can you think of more examples to give? The last sentence is a very good summary of the essay.*

5. Provide specific feedback. Don't just say the writing is good, or that it needs improvement. Tell the student specifically what they should do to improve and give them models and examples of what you expect. See **Writing Conferences: Instructional Support** on pages R54–R57 for suggested interventions.

6. Set a goal for the next conference. For example: *For our next assignment, let's work on end punctuation.*

7. Use the **Writing Portfolio Growth Record** on page R53 to track and monitor student growth and to record intervention.

Writing: Self-Assessment

Prior to meeting with students for writing conferences, you can have students at intermediate grade levels assess their own work.

Project or make copies of and distribute the checklist below. Model the activity before asking students to complete it themselves. Think aloud for students as you complete the steps. During the think-aloud, review the meanings of any vocabulary that may be unfamiliar to ELLs (e.g., *prompt*, *restate*, *summarize*).

Show students how to use a dictionary, and provide dictionaries for students to use as they assess their work.

Writing: Self-Assessment Checklist

Name _____   Date _____

Directions: Use this checklist to revise and improve your writing.

1. Read your writing out loud quietly to yourself.

☐ Does the writing make sense?

☐ Does the writing answer the prompt?

2. Does the topic sentence restate the prompt?

_____ yes _____ no

3. Are there three examples to support your topic sentence?

Name them: _____

_____

_____

4. Does the last sentence summarize the writing?

_____ yes _____ no

5. Circle spelling, punctuation, or capitalization errors. Correct the errors. Use a dictionary to fix spelling errors.

Writing Portfolios

Overview

Writing portfolios are an excellent way to monitor and assess English language learners' growth in writing throughout the year—or better, over the course of several years, as the portfolios will ideally follow the students from grade to grade. Documenting growth over time is especially important because it is difficult to evaluate ELLs against grade-level norms while they are in the process of learning English.

Here are some strategies to use when implementing writing portfolios in the classroom.

Ensure writing samples are gathered throughout the year.

- Begin the year with a baseline or benchmark assessment. Choose a topic and genre that all students can relate to, such as a personal narrative about a family custom or an opinion piece of each student's choosing.

- Evaluate the writing for strengths and weaknesses and record the results. For ELLs, use a writing rubric that reflects the characteristics of writers at different English language proficiency levels, and use the level that matches each student's language proficiency. Share the evaluation results with students during writing conferences.

- If new students enter your classroom after your initial assessments are done, make sure to conduct a benchmark assessment for them as soon as possible.

- Collect writing samples at least three more times throughout the year. You may use the same prompt with all students, or different prompts as long as similar methods of measurement are used. It is often helpful to allow ELLs to choose among several prompts.

- Use a rubric to evaluate each new sample, and include the evaluation in the portfolio.

- Make sure to gather a final sample at the end of the year, and to schedule special end-of-year writing conferences so you can speak with students about their progress and achievements.

Make sure writing samples include a variety of genres.

Writing skills need to be developed across a range of genres, so be sure to include samples of all genres in the students' writing portfolios.

(continued)

Include all components of the writing process in at least one writing sample.

To accurately chart each student's writing accomplishments, make sure to include at least one writing sample that shows all steps of the writing process. This includes brainstorming, prewriting, multiple drafts, self-assessment, peer editing, and student-teacher writing conferences. This lets the student see the writing process from beginning to end and helps them identify which strategies improve their writing the most.

Add student reflections on their writing.

At the end of the year, have students look through their portfolios. As they review, have them choose the piece of writing they feel reflects their best work. Remember that students are deciding which assignments they think are their personal best. It is not a comparison to another student's writing.

Then have each student reflect on the piece of writing. The reflection can be done in a variety of ways, including:

- A letter to the teacher or parent about the work, including why the student feels the writing is his or her best.

- An oral presentation of the writing assignment, in which students reflect on the writing process, the improvements they made as a writer, and the strengths of their final draft.

Writing Portfolio Growth Record

Student _____

Date _____

Type of writing assignment _____

Strengths _____

_____

_____

Challenges _____

_____

_____

Student's goal _____

_____

_____

How will we work toward this goal? _____

_____

_____

Notes _____

_____

To the Teacher: Use this form to track student writing progress over the course of the school year. Keep this log in the student's writing portfolio.

Writing Conferences: Instructional Support

Primary Grades

The suggested interventions shown here are only samples of how a teacher might give instructional feedback to a child. Teachers will need to adjust their instructional support based on the individual needs of children.

If a child's writing features the following:	**Then** provide the following instructional support:
Sentences contain fragments and are not complete.	Practice adding words to make a complete sentence using fragments such as *my puppy* or *eats an apple*.
Sentences do not have subject/verb agreement (e.g., *My brother and I likes to play*.).	Model and directly teach subject/verb agreement using just a subject and verb, such as *I like, you like, my brother and I like, it likes*, and other subject/verb combinations.
Sentences do not contain correct use of articles *a*, *an*, and *the*.	Practice appropriate use of *a*, *an*, and *the* using pictures and sentence frames, such as *This is a _____* and *This is the _____ I want.*
Pronouns are used incorrectly (e.g., the subject is restated with a pronoun as in *My brother and I we play*.).	Model using either *My brother and I* or *We*, but not both. Practice using other examples and nonexamples and have the child select the correct form.
Prepositions are used incorrectly (e.g., *in the grass* is used instead of *on the grass*).	Practice use of prepositions using objects or cut-out shapes.
Sentences are written in present tense or present progressive tense only (e.g., *I walk* or *I am walking*).	Model and directly teach sentences that use the past and past progressive tense, such as *I walked* or *I was walking*.

Writing Conferences: Instructional Support

Primary Grades

If a child's writing features the following:	Then provide the following instructional support:
Some words are misspelled as a result of possible articulation issues (e.g., *den* instead of *then*).	Practice with minimal pairs of words, such as *den/then* and *there/dare*, emphasizing the tongue position and use of vocal chords in pronouncing each sound.
Sentences do not contain end punctuation.	Practice placing punctuation at the end of each complete thought, and point out how punctuation makes the writing easier to read and understand. Explain how to choose a period, a question mark, or an exclamation point to end a sentence.
Possessive nouns do not contain apostrophes.	Model and directly teach the use of possessives. Compare using *s* for plurals and *'s* for possessives.
Sentences are complete, but are all simple. Compound sentences are not used.	Model use of varied sentences in read-alouds. Directly teach how to combine simple sentences using a conjunction *and*, *but*, and *or*. Provide simple sentences, such as these: *I ride my bike. Mom watches me.* Practice combining the sentences to make a compound sentence.
Placement of direct and indirect objects is reversed (e.g., *I play with Anna soccer.*).	Practice sentences with direct objects, such as *I play soccer.* Then use sentence frames to teach correct placement, such as *I play _____ with _____.*
Collocations, or words that are usually used together, are used incorrectly (e.g., *I am great by reading* instead of *I am great at reading*). Note: Correct use of collocations requires an advanced level of vocabulary development acquired through familiarity.	Discuss the meaning of the collocation and provide examples of how it is typically used. Provide sentence frames to practice the use, such as *I am great at _____.*

Writing Conferences: Instructional Support

Intermediate Grades

The suggested interventions shown here are only samples of how a teacher might give instructional feedback to a student. Teachers will need to adjust their instructional support based on the individual needs of their students.

If a student's writing shows evidence of these difficulties:	**Then** provide the following instructional support:
Sentences contain fragments and are not complete.	Practice adding words to make a complete sentence using fragments such as *my puppy*, or *eats an apple*.
Sentences do not have subject/verb agreement (e.g., *My sister and I likes to cook* or *We is friends*).	Model and directly teach subject/verb agreement using just a subject and verb, such as *I like, you like, my sister and I like, we are, he is* and other subject/verb combinations.
Sentences do not contain correct use of articles *a, an,* and *the*.	Practice appropriate use of *a, an,* and *the* using pictures and sentence frames, such as *This is a* _____ and *This is the* _____ *I want*.
Pronouns are used incorrectly (e.g., the subject is restated with a pronoun as in *My brother and I we play*.).	Model using either *My brother and I* or *We*, but not both. Practice using other examples and nonexamples and have the child select the corrrect form.
Prepositions are used incorrectly (e.g., *bump on the tree* is used instead of *bump into the tree*).	Practice use of prepositions using objects in the classroom.
Sentences are written in present tense or present progressive tense only (e.g., *I walk* or *I am walking*).	Model and directly teach sentences that use the past and past progressive tense, such as *I walked* or *I was walking*. Introduce some irregular verbs, such as *teach/taught* and *keep/kept*.

Writing Conferences: Instructional Support

Intermediate Grades

If a student's writing features the following:	**Then** provide the following instructional support:
Some words are misspelled as a result of possible articulation issues (e.g., *den* instead of *then*).	Practice with minimal pairs of words, such as *den/then* and *there/dare*, emphasizing the tongue position and use of vocal chords in pronouncing each sound.
Contractions are not used correctly (e.g., *his* instead of *he's* or *were* instead of *we're*).	Directly teach contractions and point out the differences in meaning between the misused words. Practice forming contractions correctly.
Possessive nouns do not contain apostrophes.	Model and directly teach the use of possessives. Compare using *s* for plurals and *'s* for possessives.
Sentences are complete, but are all simple. Compound and complex sentences are not used.	Model use of varied sentences in read-alouds. Directly teach how to combine simple sentences using a conjunction *and*, *but*, and *or*. Provide simple sentences, such as these: *I like music. I want to play the guitar.* Practice combining the sentences to make a compound sentence. Then practice forming complex sentences.
Placement of direct and indirect objects is reversed (e.g., *I play with Anna soccer.*).	Practice sentences with direct objects, such as *I play soccer.* Then use sentence frames to teach correct placement, such as *I play _____ with _____ .*
Collocations, or words that are usually used together, are used incorrectly (e.g., *great by* instead of *great at*). Note: Correct use of collocations requires an advanced level of vocabulary development acquired through familiarity.	Discuss the meaning of the collocation and provide examples of how it is typically used. Provide sentence frames to practice the use, such as *I am great at _____ .*

Name of Writer _____

Name of Partner _____

Peer Conference Form

 Listen to your partner read.

Write what you think.

One thing I like is:

I did not understand:

One thing that could be better is:

 My favorite part is: _____

_____

 One question I have is: _____

_____

Name of Writer _____

Name of Partner _____

Peer Conference Form

LISTEN AND EVALUATE	CIRCLE ONE
1. Does the writing have a good beginning?	Yes No
2. Does the writing have facts and details?	Yes No
3. Does the writing have a good ending?	Yes No

What I like about this writing is _____

_____

_____.

I want to know more about _____

_____

_____.

Name of Writer _____

Name of Partner _____

Peer Conference Form

LISTEN AND EVALUATE	CIRCLE ONE
1. Does the writer use the words *I*, *my*, and *me?*	Yes No
2. Does the writing tell about an important event?	Yes No
3. Does the writing have details about an event?	Yes No

What I like about this writing is _____

_____

_____

I want to know more about _____

_____

_____

Name of Writer _____

Name of Partner _____

Peer Conference Form

LISTEN AND EVALUATE	CIRCLE ONE
1. Does the writing answer a question about the story?	Yes No
2. Does the writing include details or examples that support the answer?	Yes No
3. Does the ending tell how the writer felt about the story?	Yes No

What I like about this writing is _____

_____ .

I want to know more about _____

_____ .

Name of Writer _____

Name of Partner _____

Peer Conference Form

LISTEN AND EVALUATE	CIRCLE ONE
1. Does the beginning give an opinion?	Yes No
2. Does the writing include reasons that explain the writer's opinion?	Yes No
3. Does the ending repeat the writer's opinion?	Yes No

What I like about this writing is _____

_____

_____.

I want to know more about _____

_____

_____.

Name of Writer _____

Name of Responder _____

Informative Writing

LISTEN AND EVALUATE	RESPOND
Beginning 1. Does the writing have a good opening? Circle: **Yes** **No**	**For *yes:*** Good! Your writing has a good opening. **For *no:*** How can you start your writing?
Body 2. Does the writing have facts and details? Circle: **Yes** **No**	**For *yes:*** Good! Your writing has facts and details. **For *no:*** Can you write facts and details?
Ending 3. Does the writing have a good ending? Circle: **Yes** **No**	**For *yes:*** Good! Your writing has a good ending. **For *no:*** How can you end your writing?

Name of Writer _____

Name of Responder _____

Informative Writing

LISTEN AND EVALUATE	RESPOND
Beginning **1.** Does the writing start with an opening question or a topic sentence? Circle: **Yes** **No**	**For *yes:*** Good! Your writing starts with _____. **For *no:*** What _____ can you ask to begin your writing? What _____ can you write?
Body **2.** Does the writing include facts and details that support the topic? Circle: **Yes** **No**	**For *yes:*** Good! You have included _____ that support _____. **For *no:*** What _____ can you include that support _____ ?
Ending **3.** Does the writing end with a sentence that sums up the facts and details? Circle: **Yes** **No**	**For *yes:*** Good! Your writing ends with a _____ that sums up the _____. **For *no:*** How can you write _____ that sums up the _____ ?

Give the writer some more feedback. Use words from this box.

- a good introductory sentence
- important facts and details
- a good sentence at the end
- different kinds of sentences
- few errors in spelling
- few errors in punctuation

The best part of this writing is that it has _____.

The writer could make this writing better by _____

Name of Writer _____

Name of Responder _____

Peer Conference Form
ELL TEACHER'S HANDBOOK

**Intermediate Grades
High Intermediate**

Informative Writing

LISTEN AND EVALUATE	RESPOND
Beginning **1.** Does the writing start with an opening question or a topic sentence? Write **Yes** or **No:** _____	For *yes:* _____. For *no:* _____?
Body **2.** Does the writing include facts and details that support the topic? Write **Yes** or **No:** _____	For *yes:* _____. For *no:* _____?
Ending **3.** Does the writing end with a sentence that sums up the facts and details? Write **Yes** or **No:** _____	For *yes:* _____. For *no:* _____?

Give the writer some more feedback. Use words from this box.

- a good introductory sentence
- important facts and details
- a good sentence at the end

- different kinds of sentences
- few errors in spelling
- few errors in punctuation

What do I like about this writing? _____

How could this writing be improved? _____

Peer Conference Form
ELL TEACHER'S HANDBOOK

Intermediate Grades
Proficient

Name of Writer ____________________

Name of Responder ____________________

Informative Writing

LISTEN AND EVALUATE	RESPOND
Beginning **1.** Does the writing start with an opening question or a topic sentence? ____________________	**For *yes:*** ____________________ ____________________. **For *no:*** ____________________ ____________________?
Body **2.** Does the writing include facts and details that support the topic? ____________________	**For *yes:*** ____________________ ____________________. **For *no:*** ____________________ ____________________?
Ending **3.** Does the writing end with a sentence that sums up the facts and details? ____________________	**For *yes:*** ____________________ ____________________. **For *no:*** ____________________ ____________________?

Give the writer some more feedback.

What do I like about this writing? ____________________

____

How could this writing be improved? ____________________

____

Name of Writer _____

Name of Responder _____

Personal Narrative

LISTEN AND EVALUATE	RESPOND
1. Does the writing use words such as *I, my,* and *me?* Circle: **Yes** **No**	**For *yes:*** Good! The writing uses words such as *I, my,* and *me.* **For *no:*** How can you use these words in your writing?
2. Does the writing tell about an important event in the person's life? Circle: **Yes** **No**	**For *yes:*** Good! The writing tells about an important event in the person's life. **For *no:*** What important event in the person's life can you tell about?
3. Does the writing have details about the event? Circle: **Yes** **No**	**For *yes:*** Good! The writing has details about the event. **For *no:*** What details can you write?

Name of Writer _____

Name of Responder _____

Personal Narrative

LISTEN AND EVALUATE	RESPOND
1. Does the writing use pronouns such as *I, my,* and *me?* Circle: **Yes** **No**	**For *yes:*** Good! The writing uses the pronouns _____. **For *no:*** What _____ did you use in your writing? How can you use _____?
2. Does the writing tell about an important or interesting event in the person's life? Circle: **Yes** **No**	**For *yes:*** Good! The writing tells about an _____. **For *no:*** What is an _____ that you can include?
3. Does the writing have details that tell about the event? Circle: **Yes** **No**	**For *yes:*** Good! The writing has _____ that tell about _____. **For *no:*** What _____ can you add that tell _____?

Give the writer some more feedback. Use words from this box.

- a good opening sentence
- interesting details about the event
- easy to understand
- a good closing sentence
- different kinds of sentences
- correct grammar
- few errors in spelling
- few errors in punctuation

The best part of this writing is that it _____

_____

The writer could make this writing better by _____

_____

Name of Writer _____

Name of Responder _____

Personal Narrative

LISTEN AND EVALUATE	RESPOND
1. Did the writing use pronouns such as *I, my,* and *me?* Write **Yes** or **No:** _____	**For *yes:*** _____ _____. **For *no:*** _____ _____?
2. Does the writing tell about an important or interesting event in the person's life? Write **Yes** or **No:** _____	**For *yes:*** _____ _____. **For *no:*** _____ _____?
3. Does the writing have details that tell about the event? Write **Yes** or **No:** _____	**For *yes:*** _____ _____. **For *no:*** _____ _____?

Give the writer some more feedback. Use words from this box.

- a good opening sentence
- interesting details about the event
- easy to understand
- different kinds of sentences
- correct grammar and spelling
- a good closing sentence

What do I like about this writing? _____

How could this writing be improved? _____

Name of Writer _____

Name of Responder _____

Personal Narrative

LISTEN AND EVALUATE	RESPOND
1. Does the writer use pronouns such as *I, my,* and *me?* _____	**For *yes:*** _____ _____. **For *no:*** _____ _____?
2. Does the writing tell about an important or interesting event in the person's life? _____	**For *yes:*** _____ _____. **For *no:*** _____ _____?
3. Does the writing have details that clearly describe the event? _____	**For *yes:*** _____ _____. **For *no:*** _____ _____?

Give the writer some more feedback.

What do I like about this writing? _____

_____

How could this writing be improved? _____

_____

Name of Writer _____

Name of Responder _____

Response to Literature

LISTEN AND EVALUATE	RESPOND
Beginning **1.** Does the response answer the question about the story? Circle: **Yes** **No**	**For *yes:*** Good! The response answers the question about the story. **For *no:*** What is the answer to the question?
Body **2.** Does the response have details or examples? Circle: **Yes** **No**	**For *yes:*** Good! You have details or examples. **For *no:*** What details or examples can you write?
Ending **3.** Does the last sentence tell how the writer feels about the story? Circle: **Yes** **No**	**For *yes:*** Good! Your last sentence tells how you feel about the story. **For *no:*** Try to write a sentence that tells how you feel about the story.

Peer Conference Form
ELL TEACHER'S HANDBOOK

**Intermediate Grades
Early Intermediate**

Response to Literature

LISTEN AND EVALUATE	RESPOND
Beginning **1.** Does the response answer the question about the story? Circle: **Yes** **No** Does it give an opinion about the story? Circle: **Yes** **No**	**For *yes:*** Good! The response answers the _____. It gives an _____ about the story. **For *no:*** What is the answer to the _____? How can you give an _____ about the story?
Body **2.** Does the response include details or examples that support the answer? Circle: **Yes** **No**	**For *yes:*** Good! You've included _____ or _____ that support your _____. **For *no:*** What _____ or _____ can you include that support _____?
Ending **3.** Does the last sentence sum up how the writer felt about the story? Circle: **Yes** **No**	**For *yes:*** Good! Your last sentence sums up _____. **For *no:*** How do you _____ about the story? Try to write a _____ that sums up _____.

Give the writer some more feedback. Use words from the box.

- support your opinion
- details that tell why
- examples that explain why
- correct grammar and spelling

The best part of this response is that it gives _____.

The writer could make this response better by including _____.

Name of Writer _____

Name of Responder _____

Response to Literature

LISTEN AND EVALUATE	RESPOND
Beginning 1. Does the response answer the question about the story? Write **Yes** or **No**: _____ Does it give an opinion about the story? Write **Yes** or **No**: _____	For *yes:* _____ _____. For *no:* _____ _____?
Body 2. Does the response include details or examples that support the answer? Write **Yes** or **No**: _____	For *yes:* _____. For *no:* _____?
Ending 3. Does the last sentence sum up how the writer felt about the story? Write **Yes** or **No**: _____	For *yes:* _____. For *no:* _____?

Give the writer some more feedback. Use words from this box.

- support your opinion
- details that tell why
- examples that explain why
- correct grammar and spelling

What do I like about this response? _____

How could this response be improved? _____

Peer Conference Form
ELL TEACHER'S HANDBOOK

**Intermediate Grades
Proficient**

Response to Literature

LISTEN AND EVALUATE	RESPOND
Beginning **1.** Does the response answer the question about the story? Does it give an opinion about the story? _____	For *yes:* _____ _____. For *no:* _____ _____?
Body **2.** Does the response include details or examples that support the answer? _____	For *yes:* _____ _____. For *no:* _____ _____?
Ending **3.** Does the last sentence sum up how the writer felt about the story? _____	For *yes:* _____ _____. For *no:* _____ _____?

Give the writer some more feedback.

What do I like about this response? _____

_____

How could this response be improved? _____

_____

Name of Writer _____

Name of Responder _____

Opinion Writing

LISTEN AND EVALUATE	RESPOND
1. Does the first sentence tell an opinion, or what the writer thinks? Circle: **Yes** **No**	**For *yes:*** Good! The first sentence tells what you think. **For *no:*** What do you think about the topic?
2. Does the writing have reasons that explain the writer's opinion? Circle: **Yes** **No**	**For *yes:*** Good! You have reasons that tell what you think. **For *no:*** What reasons can you give to explain what you think?
3. Does the last sentence tell what the writer thinks again? Circle: **Yes** **No**	**For *yes:*** Good! Your last sentence tells what you think again. **For *no:*** Try to write a sentence that tells what you think again.

Name of Writer _____

Name of Responder _____

Opinion Writing

LISTEN AND EVALUATE	RESPOND
1. Does the first sentence tell the writer's opinion about a topic and use the words *in my opinion?* Circle: **Yes** **No**	**For *yes:*** Good! The first sentence tells your _____. It uses the words _____. **For *no:*** What is your _____ about the topic? How can you use the words _____?
2. Does the writing include reasons that explain the opinion? Circle: **Yes** **No**	**For *yes:*** Good! You've included _____ that explain your _____. **For *no:*** What _____ can you include that explain your _____?
3. Does the writing end with a sentence that repeats the writer's opinion? Circle: **Yes** **No**	**For *yes:*** Good! Your writing ends with a _____ that repeats _____. **For *no:*** What is your _____? Try to write a _____ that repeats your _____.

Give the writer some more feedback. Use words from the box.

- opinion about the topic
- used the words *in my opinion*
- reasons that tell why
- a good sentence at the end
- correct grammar
- few errors in spelling and punctuation

The best part of this writing is that it gives _____

The writer could make this writing better by having _____

Name of Writer _____

Name of Responder _____

Opinion Writing

LISTEN AND EVALUATE	RESPOND
1. Does the first sentence tell the writer's opinion about a topic and use the words *in my opinion?* Write **Yes** or **No:** _____	**For *yes:*** _____ _____. **For *no:*** _____ _____?
2. Does the writing include reasons that explain the opinion? Write **Yes** or **No:** _____	**For *yes:*** _____ _____. **For *no:*** _____ _____?
3. Does the writing end with a sentence that repeats the writer's opinion? Write **Yes** or **No:** _____	**For *yes:*** _____ _____. **For *no:*** _____ _____?

Give the writer some more feedback. Use words from the box.

- opinion about the topic
- used the words *in my opinion*
- reasons that tell why
- good reasons

- a good sentence at the end
- correct grammar
- few errors in spelling
- few errors in punctuation

What do I like about this writing? _____

How could this writing be improved? _____

Name of Writer _____

Name of Responder _____

Opinion Writing

LISTEN AND EVALUATE	RESPOND
1. Does the first sentence tell the writer's opinion about a topic and use the words *in my opinion?* _____	For *yes:* _____. For *no:* _____?
2. Does the writing include reasons that explain the opinion? _____	For *yes:* _____. For *no:* _____?
3. Does the writing end with a sentence that repeats the writer's opinion? _____	For *yes:* _____. For *no:* _____?

Give the writer some more feedback.

What do I like about this writing? _____

_____

How could this writing be improved? _____

_____

English/Spanish Cognates

Helping Spanish speakers recognize cognates of English words can greatly increase ELLs' reading vocabulary and understanding of instructional and academic language. It is important to note, however, that students who have limited or interrupted prior formal schooling may not know the meanings of the Spanish cognates of some of these words.

False Cognates

Warn students to beware of "false cognates," words that have similar forms in both languages, but different meanings. Here are a few common examples:

- *ropa* means *clothing*, not *rope*
- *sopa* means *soup*, not *soap*
- *campo* means *field*, not *camp*
- *largo* means *long*, not *large*

English	Spanish
accident	accidente
activity	actividad
adult	adulto
adventure	aventura
air	aire
alarm	alarma
alphabet	alfabeto
ambulance	ambulancia
animal	animal
appetite	apetito
April	abril
area	area
artist	artista
atlas	atlas
attention	atención
August	agosto
author	autor
avenue	avenida
balcony	balcón
banana	banana
bank	banco
bicycle	bicicleta
boat	bote
border	borde
boxer	boxeador
cable	cable
cafeteria	cafetería
camel	camello
camera	camera
canary	canario
canyon	cañon
captain	capitán
cause	causa; causar
celebrate	celebrar
cement	cemento
center	centro
cereal	cereal

English	Spanish
ceremony	ceremonia
character	carácter
chimney	chimenea
circle	círculo
circular	circular
class	clase
coast	costa
coffee	café
colony	colonia
color	color
common	común
community	comunidad
compare	comparar
complete	completo/a; completar
confusing	confuso/a
continue	continuar
contrast	contraste; contrastar
coyote	coyote
crocodile	cocodrilo
culture	cultura
curious	curioso/a
dance	danza; danzar
December	diciembre
decide	decidir
decorate	decorar
decoration	decoración
depend	depender
describe	describir
desert	desierto
destroy	destruir
diamond	diamante
dictionary	diccionario
difference	diferencia
different	diferente
dinosaur	dinosaurio
direct	directo/a
direction	*dirección

English	Spanish
disaster	desastre
discuss	*discutir
discussion	discusión
distance	distancia
dollar	dólar
double	doble
electric	eléctrico/a
electricity	electricidad
elephant	elefante
energy	energía
English	inglés
enormous	enorme
enter	entrar
error	error
escape	escapar
especially	especialmente
exam	examen
examine	examinar
exclaim	exclamar
extra	extra
extraordinary	extraordinario/a
fable	fábula
fabulous	fabuloso
false	falso
family	familia
famous	famoso/a
fantasy	fantasía
favorite	favorito/a
February	febrero
final	final
finally	finalmente
flower	flor
football	*fútbol
fruit	fruta
gallon	galón
garden	jardín
gas (gasoline)	gas (gasolina)

English/Spanish Cognates (cont.)

English	Spanish	English	Spanish	English	Spanish
giant	gigante	May	mayo	project	proyecto
giraffe	jirafa	memory	memoria	quarter	cuarto; cuarto/a
group	grupo	metal	metal	ranch	rancho
guide	guía	microscope	microscopio	reality	realidad
helicopter	helicóptero	million	millón	really	realmente
history	*historia	minute	minuto	reason	razón
hospital	hospital	moment	momento	rhyme	rima; rimar
hotel	hotel	much	mucho	rhythm	ritmo
hour	hora	music	música	rich	rico/a
human	humano; humano/a	natural	natural	rock	roca
idea	idea	necessary	necesario/a	route	ruta
ideal	ideal	nervous	nervioso/a	salad	ensalada
identify	identificar	normal	normal	science	ciencias
imagine	imaginar	notice	noticia; notar	secret	secreto
immediately	inmediatamente	November	noviembre	September	septiembre
immigrant	inmigrante	object	objeto	social studies	estudios sociales
importance	importancia	observe	observar	special	especial
important	importante	occur	ocurrir	specific	específico/a
independence	independencia	ocean	océano	stomach	estómago
information	información	October	octubre	story	*historia
insect	insecto	office	oficina	study	estudiar
instructions	instrucciones	opinion	opinión	surprise	sorpresa
intelligent	inteligente	ordinary	ordinario/a	talent	talento
interesting	interesante	palace	palacio	tea	té
interrupt	interrumpir	paper	papel	telephone	teléfono
introduce	introducir	park	parque	telescope	telescopio
introduction	introducción	part	parte	television	*televisión
invent	inventar	past	pasado	temperature	temperatura
island	isla	paste	pasta	terrible	terrible
jar	jarra	patio	patio	theme	tema
July	julio	pearl	perla	theory	teoría
June	junio	penguin	pingüino	title	título
kilogram	kilogramo	perfect	perfecto/a; perfeccionar	tomato	tomate
lemon	limón	photograph	fotografía	total	total
leopard	leopardo	photographer	fotógrafo/a	totally	totalmente
lesson	lección	piano	piano	tourist	turista
letter	*letra	pirate	pirata	traffic	tráfico
line	línea	plan	plan; planear	train	tren
lion	león	planet	planeta	trumpet	trompeta
list	lista; listar	plant	planta; plantar	tube	tubo
machine	máquina	plastic	plástico; plástico/a	tunnel	túnel
magic	magia; mágico/a	plate	plato	uniform	uniforme
manner	manera	plural	plural	use	usar
map	mapa	poem	poema	vacation	vacación
march	marchar	police	policía	victory	victoria
March	marzo	practice	práctica; practicar	visit	visitar
marvelous	maravilloso/a	prepare	preparar	vocabulary	vocabulario
mathematics	matemática	problem	problema	vote	voto; votar

* *direction* is cognate only with spatial direction; instructional *directions* are *instrucciones*

* *discutir* can mean either *discuss* or *argue*.

* *fútbol* normally refers to *soccer*; *fútbol americano* is used for the kind played in the United States.

* *historia* can mean either *history* or *story*.

* *letra* is cognate only with the meaning of a letter of the alphabet; a letter you write to somebody is a *carta*.

* *televisor* is used for a *television set*.

Grammar Transfer Support

The following chart identifies areas in which speakers of various primary languages may have some difficulty in acquiring English grammar (syntax). The type of transfer error and its cause is outlined for each grammatical category.

NOUNS

Grammar Point	Type of Transfer Error in English	Language Background	Cause of Transfer Difficulty
Plural forms	omission of plural marker –s *I have five book.*	Cantonese, Haitian Creole, Hmong, Khmer, Korean, Tagalog, Vietnamese	Nouns do not change form to show the plural in the primary language.
Possessive forms	avoidance of *'s* to describe possession *the children of my sister* instead of *my sister's children*	Haitian Creole, Hmong, Khmer, Spanish, Tagalog, Vietnamese	The use of a prepositional phrase to express possession reflects the only structure or a more common structure in the primary language.
	no marker for possessive forms *house my friend* instead of *my friend's house*	Haitian Creole, Khmer, Vietnamese	A noun's owner comes after the object in the primary language.
Count versus noncount nouns	use of plural forms for English noncount nouns *the furnitures, the color of her hairs*	Haitian Creole, Russian, Spanish, Tagalog	Nouns that are count and noncount differ between English and the primary language.

ARTICLES

Grammar Point	Type of Transfer Error in English	Language Background	Cause of Transfer Difficulty
Placement of articles	omission of article *He has job. His dream is to become lawyer, not teacher.*	Cantonese, Haitian Creole, Hmong, Khmer, Korean, Russian, Tagalog, Vietnamese	Articles are either lacking or the distinction between *a* and *the* is not paralleled in the primary language.
	omission of articles in certain contexts, such as to identify a profession *He is teacher.*	Spanish	The article is not used in Spanish in this context, but it is needed in English.
Use of articles	overuse of articles *The honesty is the best policy. This food is popular in the Japan. I like the cats.*	Arabic, Haitian Creole, Hmong, Spanish, Tagalog	The article is used in the primary language in places where it isn't used in English.
	use of *one* for *a/an* *He is one engineer.*	Haitian Creole, Hmong, Vietnamese	Learners sometimes confuse the articles *a/an* with *one* since articles either do not exist in the primary language or serve a different function.

Grammar Transfer Support (cont.)

PRONOUNS

Grammar Point	Type of Transfer Error in English	Language Background	Cause of Transfer Difficulty
Personal pronouns, gender	use of pronouns with inappropriate gender *He is my sister.*	Cantonese, Haitian Creole, Hmong, Khmer, Korean, Tagalog	The third person pronoun in the primary language is gender free. The same pronoun is used where English uses masculine, feminine, and neuter pronouns, resulting in confusion of pronoun forms in English.
	use of pronouns with inappropriate gender *He is my sister.*	Spanish	In Spanish, subject pronouns are dropped in everyday speech and the verb conveys third-person agreement, effectively collapsing the two pronouns and causing transfer difficulty for subject pronouns in English.
	use of inappropriate gender, particularly with neuter nouns *The house is big. She is beautiful.*	Russian, Spanish	Inanimate nouns have feminine and masculine gender in the primary language, and the gender may be carried over into English.
Personal pronoun forms	confusion of subject and object pronoun forms *Him hit me. I like she.* *Let we go.*	Cantonese, Hmong, Khmer	The same pronoun form is used for *he/him*, *she/her*, and in some primary languages for *I/me* and *we/us*.
	use of incorrect number for pronouns *I saw many yellow flowers.* *It was pretty.*	Cantonese, Korean	There is no number agreement in the primary language.
	omission of subject pronouns *Michael isn't here. Is in school.*	Korean, Russian, Spanish	Subject pronouns may be dropped in the primary language and the verb ending supplies information on number and/or gender.
	omission of object pronouns *That man is very rude, so nobody likes.*	Korean, Vietnamese	Direct objects are frequently dropped in the primary language.
	omission of pronouns in clauses *If not have jobs, they will not have food.*	Cantonese, Vietnamese	A subordinate clause at the beginning of a sentence does not require a subject in the primary language.
	use of pronouns with subject nouns *This car it runs very fast.* *Your friend he seems so nice.* *My parents they live in Vietnam.*	Hmong, Spanish, Vietnamese	This type of redundant structure reflects the popular "topic-comment" approach used in the primary language: The speaker mentions a topic and then makes a comment on it.

PRONOUNS *continued*

Grammar Point	Type of Transfer Error in English	Language Background	Cause of Transfer Difficulty
Pronoun use	avoidance of pronouns by repetition of nouns *Sara visits her grandfather every Sunday, and Sara makes a meal.*	Korean, Vietnamese	It is common in the primary language to repeat nouns rather than to use pronouns.
Pronoun *one*	omission of the pronoun *one* *I saw two nice cars, and I like the small.*	Russian, Spanish, Tagalog	Adjectives can be used on their own in the primary language, whereas English often requires a noun or *one*.
Possessive forms	confusion of possessive forms *The book is my.*	Cantonese, Hmong, Vietnamese	Cantonese and Hmong speakers tend to omit final *n*, creating confusion between *my* and *mine*.

ADJECTIVES

Grammar Point	Type of Transfer Error in English	Language Background	Cause of Transfer Difficulty
Placement of adjective	position of adjectives after nouns *I read a book interesting.*	Haitian Creole, Hmong, Khmer, Spanish, Vietnamese	Adjectives commonly come after nouns in the primary language.
	position of adjectives before certain pronouns *This is interesting something.*	Cantonese, Korean	Adjectives always come before words they modify in the primary language.
Comparison	omission of markers for comparison *She is smart than me.*	Khmer	Since there are no suffixes or inflections in Khmer, the tendency is to omit them in English.
	avoidance of *-er* and *-est* endings *I am more old than my brother.*	Hmong, Khmer, Korean, Spanish	Comparative and superlative are usually formed with separate words in the primary language, the equivalent of *more* and *most* in English.
Confusion of *-ing* **and** *-ed* **forms**	confusion of *-ing* and *-ed* forms *The movie was bored.* *I am very interesting in sports.*	Cantonese, Khmer, Korean, Spanish	The adjective forms in the primary language that correspond to the ones in English do not have active and passive meanings. In Korean, for many adjectives, the same form is used for both active and passive meanings, such as *boring* versus *bored*.

Grammar Transfer Support (cont.)

VERBS

Grammar Point	Type of Transfer Error in English	Language Background	Cause of Transfer Difficulty
Present tense	omission of s in present tense, third person agreement *She go to school every day.*	Cantonese, Haitian Creole, Hmong, Khmer, Korean, Tagalog, Vietnamese	There is no subject-verb agreement in the primary language.
	problems with irregular subject-verb agreement *Sue and Ed has a new house.*	Cantonese, Hmong, Khmer, Korean, Tagalog	Verb forms do not change to indicate the number of the subject in the primary language.
Past tense	omission of tense markers *I study English yesterday.* *I give it to him yesterday.*	Cantonese, Haitian Creole, Hmong, Khmer, Korean, Tagalog, Vietnamese	Verbs in the primary language do not change form to express tense.
	confusion of present form and simple past of irregular verbs *I give it to him yesterday.*	Cantonese, Spanish	Speakers of the primary language have difficulty recognizing that merely a vowel shift in the middle of the verb, rather than a change in the ending of the verb, is sufficient to produce a change of tense in irregular verbs.
Future tense	incorrect use of present for the future *I come tomorrow.*	Cantonese, Korean	The primary language allows the use of present tense for the future.
In negative statements	omission of helping verbs in negative statements *I no understand.* *I not get into university.*	Cantonese, Korean, Russian, Spanish, Tagalog	Helping verbs are not used in negative statements in the primary language.
Perfect tenses	avoidance of present perfect where it should be used *I live here for two years.*	Haitian Creole, Russian, Tagalog, Vietnamese	The verb form either doesn't exist in the primary language or has a different function.
	use of present perfect where past perfect should be used *Yesterday I have done that.*	Khmer, Korean	In the primary language a past marker, e.g., *yesterday*, is inserted to indicate a completed action and no other change is necessary. In English when a past marker is used, the verb form must change to past perfect instead of present perfect.
Past continuous	use of past continuous for recurring action in the past *When I was young, I was studying a lot.*	Korean, Spanish, Tagalog	In the primary language, the past continuous form can be used in contexts in which English uses the expression *used to* or the simple past.
Verb as a noun	omission of infinitive marker *to* *Criticize people is not good.*	Cantonese	Unlike English, Cantonese does not require an infinitive marker when using a verb as a noun.

VERBS *continued*

Grammar Point	Type of Transfer Error in English	Language Background	Cause of Transfer Difficulty
Two verbs in a sentence	Use of two or more main verbs in one clause without any connectors *I took a book studied at the library.*	Hmong	In Hmong verbs can be connected without *and* or any other conjunction (serial verbs).
Linking verbs	Omission of linking verb *He hungry.*	Cantonese, Haitian Creole, Hmong, Khmer, Russian, Vietnamese	The verb *be* is not required in all sentences. In some primary languages, it is implied in the adjectival form. In others, the concept is expressed as a verb.
Passive voice	Omission of helping verb *be* in passive voice *The food finished.*	Cantonese, Vietnamese	Passive voice in the primary language does not require a helping verb.
	Avoidance of passive constructions *They speak Creole here.* *One speaks Creole here.* avoiding the alternate *Creole is spoken here.*	Haitian Creole	Passive constructions do not exist in Haitian Creole.
Transitive verbs versus intransitive verbs	confusion of transitive and intransitive verbs *He married with a nice girl.*	Cantonese, Korean, Russian, Spanish, Tagalog	Verbs that do and do not take a direct object differ between English and the primary language.
Phrasal verbs	confusion of related phrasal verbs *I look after the word in the dictionary.* instead of *I look up the word in the dictionary.*	Korean, Russian, Spanish	Phrasal verbs do not exist in the primary language. There is often confusion over their meanings in English.
have **versus** *be*	use of *have* instead of *be* *I have hunger. I have right.*	Spanish	Some Spanish constructions use *have* where English uses *be*.

ADVERBS

Grammar Point	Type of Transfer Error in English	Language Background	Cause of Transfer Difficulty
Use of adverbs	use of adjective form where adverb form is needed *Walk quiet.*	Haitian Creole, Hmong, Khmer	There are no suffix-derived adverb forms in the primary language, and the adjective form is used after the verb.
Placement of adverbs	placement of adverbs before verbs *At ten o'clock this morning my plane landed.* avoiding the alternate, *My plane landed at ten o'clock this morning.*	Cantonese, Korean	Adverbs usually come before verbs in the primary language, and this tendency is carried over into English.

Grammar Transfer Support (cont.)

PREPOSITIONS

Grammar Point	Type of Transfer Error in English	Language Background	Cause of Transfer Difficulty
Preposition use	omission of prepositions *Money does not grow trees.*	Cantonese	There are no exact equivalents of English prepositions in Cantonese although there are words to mark location and movement.

COMPLEX SENTENCES

Grammar Point	Type of Transfer Error in English	Language Background	Cause of Transfer Difficulty
Relative clauses	omission of relative pronouns *My grandfather was a generous man helped everyone.*	Vietnamese	Relative pronouns are not required in Vietnamese.
	incorrect pronoun used to introduce a relative clause *the house <u>who</u> is big*	Hmong	Hmong uses the same forms of relative pronouns for both personal and inanimate antecedents.
Adverbial clauses	inclusion of additional connecting word *Because he was reckless, <u>so</u> he caused an accident.* *Although my parents are poor, <u>but</u> they are very generous.*	Cantonese, Korean, Vietnamese	The primary language sometimes uses a "balancing word" in the main clause.
	use of inconsistent tenses in sentences with multiple clauses *She <u>speaks</u> French before she <u>studied</u> English.* *After she <u>comes</u> home, it <u>was</u> raining.* *We <u>will go</u> to the beach if the weather <u>will be</u> nice.*	Cantonese, Hmong, Tagalog, Vietnamese	The primary language lacks tense markers so that matching the tenses of two verbs in one sentence correctly can be difficult. Learners may also try to analyze the tense needed in English according to meaning, which in some cases can result in the use of an incorrect tense.
If **versus** *when*	Confusion of *if* and *when* *If you get there, call me!* instead of *When you get there, call me!*	Korean	The primary language has one expression that covers the use of English *if* and *when* for the future.

INFINITIVES AND GERUNDS

Grammar Point	Type of Transfer Error in English	Language Background	Cause of Transfer Difficulty
Infinitive and gerund use	use of present tense verbs in places where gerunds or infinitives are used in English *Stop walk.* *I want go there.*	Haitian Creole, Khmer, Korean	Either the *–ing* form does not exist in the primary language, or learners tend to use present tense verbs instead of gerunds even if they do exist [Haitian Creole].
	use of *for* in infinitive phrases *They went for to see the movie.*	Spanish	Spanish uses a prepositional form in similar constructions, which is carried over into English and translated as *for*.

SENTENCE STRUCTURE

Grammar Point	Type of Transfer Error in English	Language Background	Cause of Transfer Difficulty
Objects	omission of object *He dyed [his hair].* *Yes, I want [some].*	Korean	Korean tends to omit objects and noun phrases after verbs.
Variety	lack of variety in the position of clauses *Because you weren't at home and I couldn't find you, I left.* avoiding the alternate, *I left because you weren't at home and I couldn't find you.*	Korean	Since main clauses always come last in Korean, there is a tendency to put the main clause last in English. This is not an error in English, but it leads to a lack of sentence variety.
Sequential action	clauses that describe earlier actions come first *After I finish my homework, I will watch TV.* avoiding the alternate, *I will watch TV after I finish my homework.*	Cantonese, Korean	The pattern in the primary language is to describe what happens first while later occurrences follow. This is not an error in English, but it leads to a lack of sentence variety.
Placement issues	placement of phrase with the indirect object before the direct object *They gave to the girl the book.*	Spanish	The phrase with the indirect object can come before the direct object in Spanish.
	placement of modifiers between verb and direct object *She speaks very well English.*	Korean, Spanish	Word order, including the placement of adverbials, is freer in the primary language than in English.
Usage issues	use of double negatives *I no see nobody.*	Spanish	Spanish requires double negatives in many sentence structures.
	use of clauses for other structures *I want that you help me.*	Russian, Spanish	Verbs that take direct objects versus those that require clauses differ in the primary language and English.

Grammar Transfer Support (cont.)

QUESTIONS

Grammar Point	Type of Transfer Error in English	Language Background	Cause of Transfer Difficulty
Subject-verb order	lack of subject-verb inversion in questions with helping verbs *When she will be home?* *Where you are going?*	Cantonese, Hmong, Russian, Tagalog	In the primary language, word order is the same in some questions and statements, depending on the context.
Do **and** *did*	omission of *do* or *did* in questions *Where you went?*	Haitian Creole, Hmong, Khmer, Korean, Russian, Spanish, Tagalog	In the primary language, there is no exact counterpart to the *do/did* verb in questions.
Yes/no questions	avoidance of English inverted question forms in yes/no questions in favor of tag questions or intonation *You come tomorrow, OK?* *He goes to school with you?*	Cantonese, Haitian Creole, Khmer, Korean, Russian, Tagalog, Vietnamese	The primary language doesn't use subject-verb inversion in questions.
	incorrect answer form for yes/no questions *A: Do you want more food?* *B: I want.* *A: Do you have a pen?* *B: I not have.*	Cantonese, Hmong, Khmer, Korean, Russian	In the primary language, learners tend to answer *yes* by repeating the verb in the question. They tend to say *no* by using *not* and repeating the verb.
	positive answer to negative question *A: Aren't you going?* *B: Yes. (when the person is not going)*	Cantonese, Korean, Russian	The appropriate response pattern differs between the primary language and English.
Tag questions	incorrect tag questions *You want to go home, are you?*	Cantonese, Khmer, Korean, Vietnamese	The primary language has no exact counterpart to a tag question, forms them differently, or does not add *do/did* to questions.

Phonics Transfer Support for 7 Languages

Sound Transfer (Phonology)

The symbol ■ identifies areas in which these primary language speakers may have some difficulty pronouncing and perceiving spoken English. The sound may not exist in the primary language, may exist but be pronounced somewhat differently, or may be confused with another sound. Sound production and perception issues affect phonics instruction.

CONSONANTS

Sound	Spanish	Vietnamese	Hmong	Cantonese	Haitian Creole	Korean	Khmer
/b/ as in bat			■	■		■	
/k/ as in cat and kite			■				
/d/ as in dog				■		■	
/f/ as in fan						■	
/g/ as in goat			■	■		■	■
/h/ as in hen					■		
/j/ as in jacket	■	■	■	■			
/l/ as in lemon						■	
/m/ as in money							
/n/ as in nail							
/p/ as in pig			■				
/r/ as in rabbit	■		■	■	■	■	
/s/ as in sun			■				
/t/ as in teen		■	■				
/v/ as in video	■			■		■	■
/w/ as in wagon	■		■				■
/y/ as in yo-yo							
/z/ as in zebra	■			■		■	■
/kw/ as in queen			■				
/ks/ as in X ray			■	■			

SHORT VOWELS

Sound	Spanish	Vietnamese	Hmong	Cantonese	Haitian Creole	Korean	Khmer
short a as in hat	■	■		■		■	
short e as in set	■		■	■	■	■	
short i as in sit	■	■	■	■	■	■	
short o as in hot	■		■			■	
short u as in cup	■		■	■	■	■	

Phonics Transfer Support (cont.)

LONG VOWELS

Sound	Spanish	Vietnamese	Hmong	Cantonese	Haitian Creole	Korean	Khmer
long *a* as in d<u>a</u>te			■	■			
long *e* as in b<u>e</u>				■		■	
long *i* as in <u>i</u>ce				■			
long *o* as in r<u>oa</u>d			■	■			
long *u* as in tr<u>u</u>e				■		■	

VOWEL PATTERNS

Sound	Spanish	Vietnamese	Hmong	Cantonese	Haitian Creole	Korean	Khmer
oo as in b<u>oo</u>k	■	■	■		■	■	■
aw as in s<u>aw</u>	■					■	

DIPHTHONGS

Sound	Spanish	Vietnamese	Hmong	Cantonese	Haitian Creole	Korean	Khmer
oy as in b<u>oy</u>			■				
ow as in h<u>ow</u>	■						

R-CONTROLLED VOWELS

Sound	Spanish	Vietnamese	Hmong	Cantonese	Haitian Creole	Korean	Khmer
ir as in b<u>ir</u>d	■	■	■	■	■	■	■
ar as in h<u>ar</u>d	■	■	■	■	■	■	■
or as in f<u>or</u>m	■	■	■	■	■	■	■
air as in h<u>air</u>	■	■	■	■	■	■	■
ear as in h<u>ear</u>	■	■	■	■	■	■	■

CONSONANT DIGRAPHS

Sound	Spanish	Vietnamese	Hmong	Cantonese	Haitian Creole	Korean	Khmer
sh as in <u>sh</u>oe	■*	■		■			■
ch as in <u>ch</u>ain		■	■				
th as in <u>th</u>ink	■	■	■	■	■	■	■
ng as in si<u>ng</u>	■		■		■		

CONSONANT BLENDS

Sound	Spanish	Vietnamese	Hmong	Cantonese	Haitian Creole	Korean	Khmer
bl, tr, dr, etc. (start of words) as in <u>bl</u>ack, <u>tr</u>ee, <u>dr</u>ess		■	■	■		■	
ld, nt, rt, etc. (end of words) as in co<u>ld</u>, te<u>nt</u>, sta<u>rt</u>		■	■	■	■	■	■

* Spanish speakers from Mexico or Central America who also speak Nahuatl or a Mayan language will be familiar with this sound, written as an x in words like *mixteca* (pronounced *mishteca*).

Sound-Symbol Transfer (Phonics)

The following chart identifies sound-symbol transfer issues for four languages that use the roman alphabet. (The remaining three do not.) The symbol ■ identifies symbols that do not represent the corresponding sound in the writing system of the primary language.

CONSONANTS

Sound	Spanish	Vietnamese	Hmong	Haitian Creole
b as in <u>b</u>at			■	
c as in <u>c</u>at		■	■	■
as in <u>c</u>ent		■	■	
d as in <u>d</u>og				
f as in <u>f</u>ish				
g as in <u>g</u>oat			■	
as in <u>g</u>iant	■		■	
h as in <u>h</u>en	■			
j as in <u>j</u>acket	■	■	■	
k as in <u>k</u>ite			■	
l as in <u>l</u>emon				
m as in <u>m</u>oon				
n as in <u>n</u>ice				
p as in <u>p</u>ig				
qu as in <u>qu</u>een	■		■	■
r as in <u>r</u>abbit	■		■	
s as in <u>s</u>un			■	
t as in <u>t</u>een			■	
v as in <u>v</u>ideo	■			
w as in <u>w</u>agon		■	■	
x as in <u>X</u> ray		■	■	■
y as in <u>y</u>o-<u>y</u>o	■			
z as in <u>z</u>ebra	■	■	■	

CONSONANT DIGRAPHS

Sound	Spanish	Vietnamese	Hmong	Haitian Creole
sh as in <u>sh</u>oe	■			
ch as in <u>ch</u>air				■
th as in <u>th</u>ink as in <u>th</u>at	■			■

Phonics Transfer Support (cont.)

VOWELS AND VOWEL PATTERNS

Sound	Spanish	Vietnamese	Hmong	Haitian Creole
a as in b<u>a</u>t	■		■	
aCe as in d<u>a</u>te	■	■		
ai as in r<u>ai</u>n	■	■	■	■
ay as in d<u>ay</u>	■		■	■
au as in <u>au</u>thor	■	■	■	■
aw as in s<u>aw</u>	■	■	■	■
e as in b<u>e</u>t	■		■	■
ee as in s<u>ee</u>d	■	■	■	■
ea as in t<u>ea</u>	■	■	■	■
ew as in f<u>ew</u>	■	■	■	■
i as in s<u>i</u>t	■		■	■
iCe as in p<u>i</u>pe	■	■	■	■
o as in h<u>o</u>t	■		■	■
oCe as in r<u>o</u>de	■	■	■	■
oo as in m<u>oo</u>n	■	■	■	■
oo as in b<u>oo</u>k	■		■	■
oa as in b<u>oa</u>t	■	■	■	■
ow as in r<u>ow</u>	■	■	■	■
ow as in h<u>ow</u>	■	■	■	■
ou as in s<u>ou</u>nd	■	■	■	■
oi as in b<u>oi</u>l			■	■
oy as in b<u>oy</u>		■	■	■
u as in c<u>u</u>p	■	■	■	■
uCe as in J<u>u</u>ne	■	■		
ui as in s<u>ui</u>t	■	■	■	■
ue as in bl<u>ue</u>	■	■	■	■
y as in tr<u>y</u>	■	■	■	■
ar as in st<u>ar</u>			■	■
er as in f<u>er</u>n	■		■	■
ir as in b<u>ir</u>d	■		■	
or as in t<u>or</u>n	■		■	
ur as in b<u>ur</u>n	■		■	

Word Study Transfer Support

Spanish

English and Spanish share some basic linguistic characteristics, such as using word parts like prefixes and suffixes and changing verb forms. The example words below are not intended to be cognates, but words that illustrate the similar meanings of the word parts. Note that Haitian Creole, Cantonese, Hmong, and Vietnamese do not use word parts to construct new words in the same way that English does.

PREFIXES

English Word Part or Parts	English Example Words	Spanish Word Part or Parts	Spanish Example Words	Word Part Purpose
un-, non-, in-, dis-	unhappy nonstop incorrect dislike	in-, des-/dis- no plus the verb sin plus the noun or verb	infeliz, incorrecto desconocido disparejo no gustar sin parar	Means "not"
re-	redo	re-	rehacer	Means "again"
pre-	preteen	pre-	preescolar	Means "before"

SUFFIXES

English Word Part or Parts	English Example Words	Spanish Word Part or Parts	Spanish Example Words	Word Part Purpose
-ful	powerful	-oso/a	poderoso/a	Means "with"; turns a noun into an adjective
-able	readable likeable	-ible -able	legible agradable	Turns a verb into an adjective
-less	fearless careless	sin plus the noun prefix des-	sin miedo descuidado	Means "without"; turns a noun into an adjective
-ness	happiness	-idad	felicidad	Turns an adjective into a noun
-ion/-tion, -ment	reaction payment amazement	-ción/-sión verb stem + -o	reacción conclusión pago asombro	Turns a verb into a noun
-ly	quickly	-mente	rápidamente	Turns an adjective into an adverb

Bibliography

Arias, M.B., Ph.D., & Morillo-Campbell, M., Ph.D. (2008). *Promoting ELL Parental Involvement: Challenges in Contested Times*. Education Public Interest Center. Tempe, AZ: Arizona State University.

August, D., & Hakuta, K. (1998). *Educating Language-Minority Children*. National Research Council: Institute of Medicine. Washington, DC: National Academy Press.

August, D., & Shanahan, T. (2006). *Executive Summary: Developing Literacy in Second-Language Learners: Report of the National Literacy Panel on Language-Minority Children and Youth*. Mahwah, NJ: Lawrence Erlbaum Associates.

Calderón, M., Slavin, R., & Sánchez, M. (2011). Effective instruction for English learners. *The Future of Children*, 21 (1), 103–127.

Cipriani-Sklar, Dr. R. (2011). Generating enriched literacy experiences for older English language learners. *Reaching Reluctant Readers*. 1 (1). New York, NY: Random House.

Common Core State Standards Initiative. *Application of Common Core State Standards for English Language Learners*. Retrieved on December 19, 2011 from http://www.corestandards.org/assets/application-for-english-learners.pdf.

Cooperstein, S.E., & Kocevar-Weidinger, E. (2004). Beyond active learning: a constructivist approach to learning. *Reference Services Review*, 32 (2), 141–148.

Course Crafters, Inc. (2011). *Teaching English Language Learners: Practical Articles for Educators from The ELL Outlook™*. Haverhill, MA: Course Crafters.

Echevarria, J., Vogt, M.E., & Short, D. (2012). *Making Content Comprehensible for English Language Learners: The SIOP Model*. Needham Heights, MA: Allyn & Bacon.

Fothergrill, L. (2006). *Generating Questions: Using Critical Thinking Skills*. Retrieved on December 19, 2011 from http://www.colorincolorado.org/article/13348/.

Francis, D., Rivera, M., Lesaux, N., Kieffer, M., & Rivera, H. (2006). *Practical Guidelines for the Education of English Language Learners: Research-Based Recommendations for Instruction and Academic Interventions*. Portsmouth, NH: RMC Research Corporation, Center on Instruction.

Freeman, Y., & Freeman, D. (2009). *Academic Language for English Language Learners and Struggling Readers: How to Help Students Succeed Across Content Areas*. Portsmouth, NH: Heinemann.

Gersten, R., Baker, S.K., Shanahan, T., Linan-Thompson, S., Collins, P., & Scarcella, R. (2007). *Effective Literacy and English Language Instruction for English Learners in the Elementary Grades: A Practice Guide*. Washington, DC: National Center for Education Evaluation and Regional Assistance, Institute of Education Sciences, U. S. Department of Education.

Goldenberg, C. (2008). Teaching English language learners: what the research does—and does not—say. *American Educator*, 32 (2).

Gottlieb, M. (2006). *Assessing English Language Learners: Bridges from Language Proficiency to Academic Achievement*. Thousand Oaks, CA: Sage Publications.

Haynes, J., & Zacarian, D. (2010). *Teaching English Language Learners Across the Content Areas*. Alexandria, VA: ASCD.

NAEP. (2011). National Assessment of Educational Progress. *2011 Reading Assessment*. Retrieved on December 19, 2011 from http://nces.ed.gov/nationsreportcard/.

NCELA. (2010). The growing number of English learner students. Retrieved on March 17, 2011 from http://www.ncela.gwu.edu/files/uploads/9/growingLEP_0708.pdf.

Ovando, C., Collier, V., & Combs, M. (2003). *Bilingual and ESL Classrooms: Teaching Multicultural Contexts* (3rd ed.). Boston, MA: McGraw-Hill.

Pierce, L.V. (2002). Performance-based assessment: promoting achievement for English language learners. *ERIC/CLL News Bulletin*, 26 (1).

U.S. Census Bureau. 2011. *Statistical Abstract of the United States: 2012* (131st ed.). Retrieved on December 19, 2011 from http://www.census.gov/compendia/statab/.

U.S. Department of Education. (2002). *No Child Left Behind: Title I and Title III. P.L. 107-110*. Retrieved on December 19, 2011 from http://www2.ed.gov/policy/elsec/leg/esea02/index.html.

U.S. Department of Education, Office of English Language Acquisition, Language Enhancement, and Academic Achievement for Limited English Proficient Students. (2008). *Biennial Report to Congress on the Implementation of Title III State Formula Grant Program, School Years 2004-06*. Retrieved on December 19, 2011 from www.ncela.gwu.edu/files/uploads/3/Biennial_Report_0406.pdf.

Additional Resources

Bardovi-Harlig, K. (2000). Tense and Aspect in Second Language Acquisition: Form, Meaning, and Use. *Language Learning Monograph Series*. Malden, MA: Blackwell.

Bear, D., Helman, L., Invernizzi, M., Templeton, S., & Johnston, F. (2007). *Words Their Way with English Learners*. Upper Saddle River, NJ: Merrill Prentice Hall.

Diaz-Rico, L.T., & Weed, K.Z. (2010). *Crosscultural, Language, and Academic Development Handbook: A Complete K-12 Reference Guide* (4th ed.). Needham Heights, MA: Allyn & Bacon.

Echevarria, J., & Vogt, M.E. (2007). *99 Ideas and Activities for Teaching English Learners with the SIOP Model*. Needham Heights, MA: Allyn & Bacon.

English Language Learners: Boosting Academic Achievement. (2004). *Research Points: Essential Information for Education Policy*. Winter: Vol. 2, Issue 1. Washington, DC: American Educational Research Association.

García, G.G., & Beltrán, D. (2003). Revisioning the Blueprint: Building for the Academic Success of English Learners. In G. G. García (Ed.), *English Learners* (pp. 197–226). Newark, DE: International Reading Association.

Irujo, S. (2007). What does research tell us about teaching reading to English language learners? *The ELL Outlook*, 6 (1).

Kagan, S., & High, J. (2002). Kagan Structures for English Language Learners. *ESL Magazine*, July/August, 5 (4), 10–12.

Kagan, S., & Kagan, M. (1994). *Kagan Cooperative Learning* (2nd ed.). San Clemente, CA: Kagan Publishing.

Lesaux, N.K., Kieffer, M.J., Faller, S.E., & Kelley, J.G. (2010). The effectiveness and ease of implementation of an academic English vocabulary intervention for linguistically diverse students in urban middle schools. *Reading Research Quarterly*, 45, 196–228.

Moughamian, A.C., Rivera, M.O., & Francis, D.J. (2009). *Instructional models and strategies for teaching English language learners*. Portsmouth, NH: RMC Research Corporation, Center on Instruction.

National Reading Panel. (2000). *Teaching Children to Read: An Evidence-Based Assessment of the Scientific Research Literature on Reading and Its Implications for Reading Instruction* (NIH Publication No. 00-4769). Washington, DC: National Institute of Child Health and Human Development.

Rivera, M.O., Francis, D.J., Fernandez, M., Moughamian, A.C., Lesaux, N.K., & Jergensen, J. (2010). *Effective practices for English Language Learners. Principals from five states speak*. Portsmouth, NH: RMC Research Corporation, Center on Instruction.

Rivera, M.O., Moughamian, A.C., Lesaux, N.K., & Francis, D.J. (2009). *Language and Reading Interventions for English Language Learners and English Language Learners with Disabilities*. Portsmouth, NH: RMC Research Corporation, Center on Instruction.

Scarcella, R. (2003). *Accelerating Academic English: A Focus on English Language Learners*. Oakland, CA: Regents of the University of California.

Schleppegrell, M. (2001). Linguistic features of the language of schooling. *Linguistics and Education*, 12, 431–459.

Short, D.J., & Fitzsimmons, S. (2007). *Double the Work: Challenges and Solutions to Acquiring Language and Academic Literacy for Adolescent English Language Learners*. New York, NY: Alliance for Excellent Education.